The Sustainable Design Book

Laurence King Publishing

The Sustainable Design Book

Rebecca Proctor

Published in 2015 by
Laurence King Publishing Ltd
361–363 City Road, London
EC1V 1LR, United Kingdom
T +44 (0)20 7841 6900
enquiries@laurenceking.com
www.laurenceking.com

A catalogue record for this book is available from the British Library

ISBN: 978-1-78067-473-5

Design by Praline
Cover by Stuart Dando

Printed in the UK

Laurence King Publishing is committed to ethical and sustainable
production. We are proud participants in The Book Chain Project ®
bookchainproject.com

Front cover: Lollygagger Lounge by Loll Designs
Back cover: Box Day Bed by Mark Tuckey
Frontispiece: Transformed Stacking Vessel by Utopia and Utility

Contents

Introduction

The concept of sustainability is more popular than ever, and although we hear the words all the time, what does 'sustainable' actually mean? Does it concern ecology and the environment? Is it about people and culture or plants and animals, jobs and money? The complicated reality is that sustainability is about all of these things and more.

The term 'sustainability' was first used in forestry and in this context describes responsible stewardship of woodlands, where timber is not removed faster than the rate at which it can be regenerated. This definition can still be broadly applied to the world at large, where the ecosystem and its resources struggle to keep pace with the exploitation of materials to create products and our built environment.

In terms of sustainability and design, it can seem difficult to reconcile these two areas. Surely, if we are truly concerned about sustainability we should just stop making things, especially when it seems there is nothing wrong with what we already have? Is there really a need for constant growth and consumption?

To me however, these notions seem to fly in the face of what it is to be human. For many people there is a natural urge to design and create things, while others experience inevitable changes in circumstance that require new solutions. With this reality in mind, I personally believe that by manufacturing and consuming thoughtfully, it is possible to make sensible and inspiring choices, ultimately resulting in a positive effect on our environment.

So then, what constitutes sustainable design? In this book, I have tried to present a balanced view and show different approaches to the idea. Of course, there are recycled pieces, which use waste materials in exciting new ways, products made of biodegradable materials, organic materials and projects which engage in fair-trade initiatives. However, there are also examples of craftsmanship, stories of old traditions and new techniques.

Selection for the book was dependent on meeting several criteria. Are the products biodegradable or fairtrade? Are they recycled or recyclable? Are they made with materials that are locally sourced and well managed and finally, is their production designed to specifically limit toxins and waste? For each quality that the product has, a small icon is displayed on its page. Of course, a truly sustainable product requires the interplay of multiple factors, so most of the products have several icons listed.

Ultimately the aim of this book is to surprise, inspire and delight. I hope that by flicking through its pages you will find at least one product that will make you stop and perhaps appreciate the possibilities and profound beauty of sustainable design.

Key to Icons

To help you to see at a glance the ways in which the featured products are sustainably produced, each is accompanied by one or more of the following icons:

Biodegradeable
Applies to products that can be composted at the end of their useful life, leaving no trace of their existence.

Locally made
These products are manufactured in the same locality or country in which they are designed, benefitting the local area through employment and income, rather than exploiting cheap foreign labour.

Locally sourced
Using locally sourced materials reduces air miles, energy and packaging materials as well as helping support local industry. Many people are aware of the advantages of eating locally sourced food and the same benefits can be applied to using locally sourced materials.

Low energy
Products with this icon generally require less power to function than comparable equivalents.

Low waste
Low-waste products are either highly minimal and efficient designs, or have a system in place to reuse or recycle off-cuts and waste created in their manufacture.

No toxins
Products made from organically grown materials or products containing no harmful chemicals carry this icon.

Recyclable
If a product is recyclable, it can be turned into a fresh supply of raw material at the end of its useful life, reducing dependency on virgin resources.

Recycled
This icon indicates that a design is either wholly or in part made from materials that have been previously used. These can be either salvaged directly in their current incarnation or products from the recycling industry, such as glass, paper or metal.

Social enterprise
These products benefit society by employing disadvantaged workers and/or giving donations to charitable causes.

Traditional craftsmanship
Designs with this icon are made using skilled techniques, passed down through generations and sustaining artisanal traditions and knowledge.

Well-managed resources
Well-managed resources are materials that can be replenished at the rate they are being consumed, like bamboo, wool or sustainable timber.

A/R Studio · Alulife · Benwu Studio · Renée Boute · Bril · Clayworks · Durat · Ecovative · Lars Beller Fjetland · Elodie Gobin · Nicole Goymann · Ineke Hans · Jeongwon Ji · Mieke Meijer · Mini Moderns · Pia Design · Supercyclers · Studio Formafantasma · Usedesign · Mugi Yamamoto

Materials

Pain Brut
A/R Studio

Steel, bread

www.a-rstudio.it

Pain Brut was a very low-tech, low-cost project with a minimalist approach. Initiated by A/R Studio, the outcome of the project was a reinforced piece of bread — a poetic, flexible, resistant, fragrant material consisting of a metal net and a no-knead bread, designed to create homemade, oven-baked small objects.

An emblematic object made from this material is the Nest Box, simultaneously providing food and shelter for cold and hungry birds. When entirely eaten or damaged by weather it can be reproduced over the same net structure again and again.

Perishable and short-lived, Pain Brut addresses the contemporary concerns of ethical simplicity and sustainability.

Alulife
Alulife

100% recycled aluminium

www.alulife.com

Alulife is an innovative material, consisting of 100 per cent recycled and recyclable aluminium. As a result of an oxidation process, it takes on a complex, shimmering texture, which creates unique reflections, variations and nuances in the material.

Available as tiles or panels 3mm (⅛in) and 5mm (¼in) thick, it is suitable for both interior and exterior architecture. It is also strong, lightweight and resistant to bending and abrasion.

Alulife is available in a wide variety of colours, with both gloss and satin finishes. It can be used to create tiled walls, doors, railings, handles and furniture, as well as providing a functional element in the design of kitchen worktops. It has also been used successfully in the marine, automotive and jewellery industries. Alulife can be recycled entirely pre- and post-consumption.

Living Material
Benwu Studio
(Peng You &
Hongchao Wang)

Jesmonite, wood

www.benwustudio.com

Living Material is a project by Peng You and Hongchao Wang, the Chinese co-founders of Benwu Studio, based in London and New York. The project explores new methods of incorporating the most basic natural resources into a modern, composite material.

Living Material aims to create potential new industrial applications while also celebrating the beauty of raw ingredients such as twigs and branches. Suspending these in colourful resins, the resulting material is a unique, contrasting melding of primitive and futuristic design.

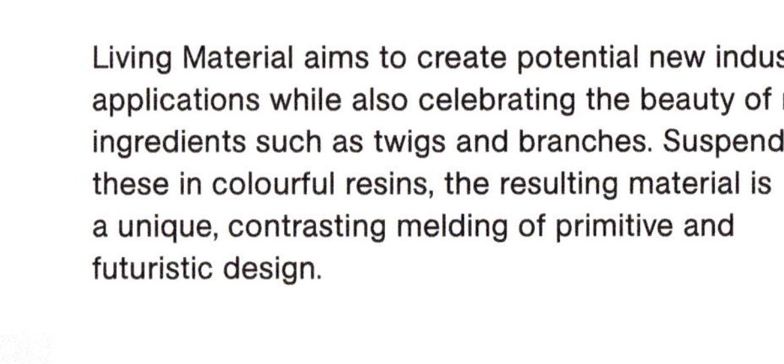

AGF Class 3
Renée Boute

Fruit and vegetables

www.reneeboute.nl

'AGF' stands for potatoes, vegetables and fruit in Dutch, while Class 3 is the category of products considered by the Dutch agricultural sector to be imperfect and therefore unsuitable for shops and supermarkets. A small number of Class 3 products are used by animal-feed producers, but the vast majority go directly on to the compost heap.

AGF Class 3 is a project by the designer Renée Boute that aims to make this waste more visible, and convince consumers of the value of these products. After much experimenting at a craft-paper mill, Boute has succeeded in producing handmade paper from various fruits and vegetables, which can be distinguished by their own unique colour, fragrance and texture.

These dried, edible sheets feature as ingredients in a cookbook that was compiled in collaboration with chef William Versteeg, and contains recipes that use rejected fruits and vegetables. The AGF Class 3 project also resulted in a limited collection of bowls made from rejected vegetables or fruit, protected against water with a natural coating.

Rammed Earthenware
Bril

Soil, sand, lime

bril.jp

Rammed earth is used as a traditional way of building walls, but Bril are investigating the use of this material for applications where structural strength is not required. Rammed Earthenware is created by filling a mould with a mixture of several colours of soil, sand, lime and water and ramming it together with wooden sticks. This is then left to air dry for several weeks before being worked with different techniques such as cutting, polishing, stamping, shaving and lathing.

The finished product is totally biodegradable; in fact the addition of lime can improve soil. The earthenware itself absorbs carbon dioxide and gets harder and harder over time, turning into a sort of limestone.

For more on Bril, see the Q&A on page 16.

Clayworks Clay Plaster
Clayworks (Adam Weismann & Katy Bryce)

Unfired clays and sands

www.clay-works.com

Clayworks Clay Plaster is a high-performance wall finish available in a wide selection of beautiful soft colours. The material aspires to replace the use of gypsums and paints while exceeding all foreseeable environmental building regulations. Made in Cornwall, England, from unfired clays and sands, the finished product takes 85 per cent less energy to create than gypsum plaster but can be composted, is non-toxic and contains no added chemicals.

Unfired clay can absorb and desorb indoor humidity faster than any other building material, and will regulate relative interior humidity to between 40 and 70 per cent, the level at which the likelihood of airborne infectious bacteria and viruses surviving is lowest. It also prevents building materials from emitting toxins such as formaldehyde, and helps prevent the occurrence of mould.

Q&A: Bril

Bril is a design collective in Japan formed by freelance designers Tatsuo Kuroda, Jo Nakamura and Fumiaki Goto. Each designer has a speciality – furniture, jewelry or crafts. While they work separately on client commissions in different places, they come together to design unique collections of experimental pieces.

www.bril.jp

Rammed earth is one of the world's oldest building techniques. Bril applied this technique of compressing soil to make their own material and products.

In what way is your work sustainable?
One year before we released the Soil collection, we had done a ceramics project. As you know, ceramic is a material made with baking clay at high temperature. After finishing the project, we became curious about clay (soil) itself and architectural techniques using raw soil without any heat. A soil wall is one of the most sustainable objects. It can be easily broken down and be rebuilt just by adding water.

How would you describe your style?
Though we mainly focus on materials as a topic, we are curious not only about a material itself, but also the stories behind the material. We investigate the stories first and try to apply them to design while using the material sensitively. The design also plays a role in letting people know the material stories.

What materials and techniques do you use?
We mainly deal with materials and techniques outside of mass production, and often collaborate with craftsmen who use unique local techniques.

What are you working on at the moment, and what do you hope to work on in the future?
We are researching how trees are used locally in Japan and Sweden, and designing one object from one tree — a project partly supported by a Swedish governmental agency.

Now we are based in Japan, we are investigating local histories and techniques as a subject. In the future, we hope to take large-scale issues faced by people in the world and look at them from micro-viewpoints like local histories and techniques.

Have you noticed any particular trends in sustainable design?
We think that some of the new trends in sustainable design follow trends in the food industry. For instance, like food, lots of people care where materials come from and how products are made. Therefore designers need to care about and answer these questions. Because of these trends, products will get simpler and simpler in both design and concept.

What materials or techniques do you think we'll be seeing more of in the future?
We guess that we will be seeing more natural materials. Now plant-based materials are the focus, but we will also see more materials from animals. We think that materials from such minute creatures as insects and fungi have many possibilities.

Each plate in the Rammed Earthenware collection is made from a combination of soil in various colours, pressed with sand, lime and water.

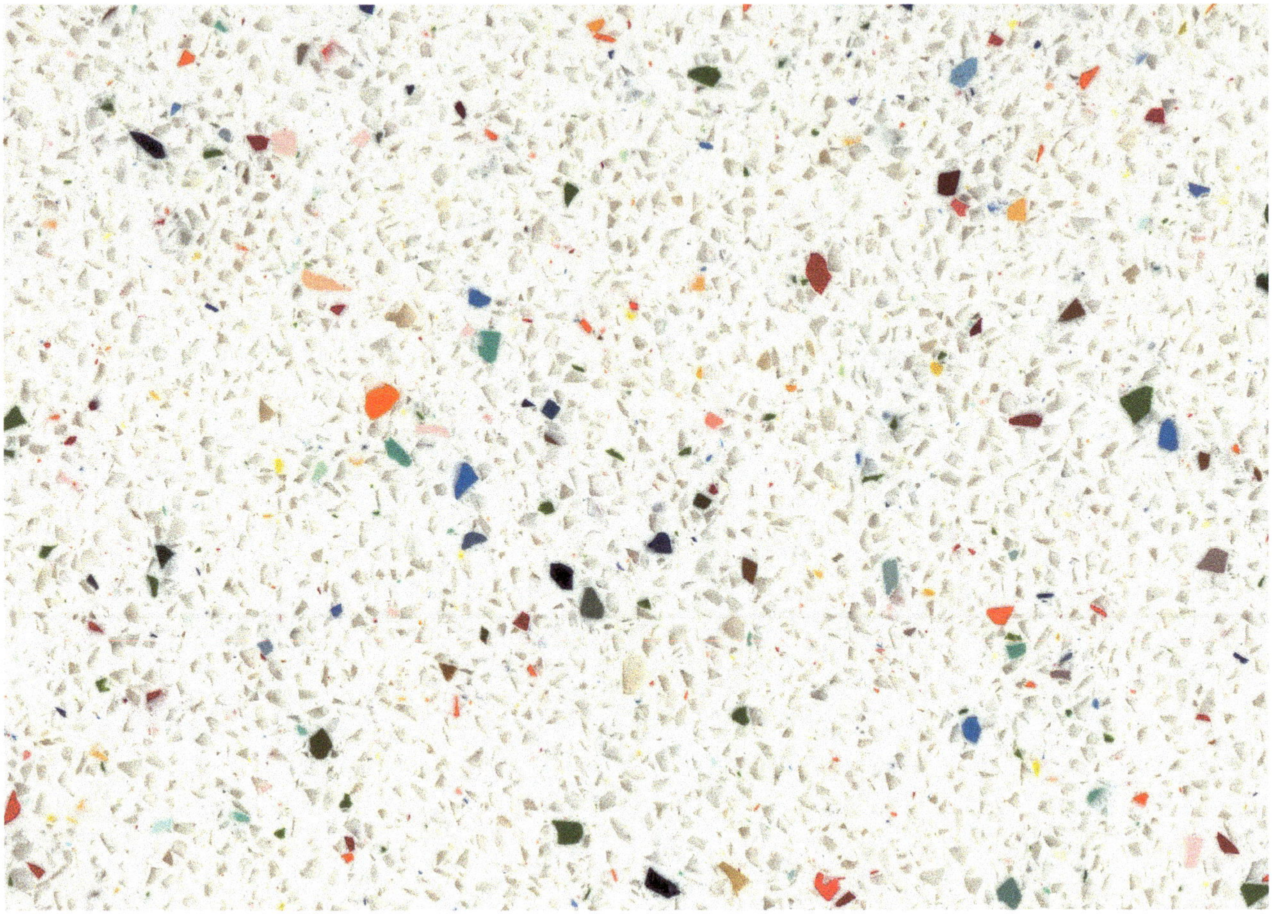

Durat
Durat

Recycled plastic

www.durat.com

Durat is a unique polyester-based, solid-surface material from Finland with a wide range of applications. It contains about 30 per cent recycled post-industrial plastic, granulated into tiny pieces, giving the material a distinctive speckled texture. The finished product is itself 100 per cent recyclable, meaning that any waste material generated can be put right back into the production line. As the name suggests, it is extremely durable and resistant to wear, humidity and chemicals. These qualities make it ideal for use in home bathrooms and kitchens, as well as restaurants, ships, hospitals and even laboratories. It can be cut, shaped and glued just like wood and the whole surface can even be renewed by light sanding.

As well as providing this raw material in a range of more than 70 colours, the company also offer a selection of geometric, minimalist ready-made items such as shower trays, sinks, tables and seating.

Ecovative
Ecovative

Mushroom mycelium

www.ecovativedesign.com

Committed to working with industry and consumers to rid the world of toxic, unsustainable materials, Ecovative is a company developing home-compostable bio-plastics based on mycelium, a living organism. Mycelium is a natural, self-assembling glue, which digests crop waste to produce cost-competitive and environmentally responsible material. This material is then used to create high-performance alternatives to traditional plastic foam packaging.

Ecovative's highly distinctive packaging aims to replace thousands of plastic foam parts and has already been adopted by sustainability leaders like Steelcase. It is also used by sports giant Puma to package a stand-up paddleboard, whose sleek and glossy black lines provide a radical contrast to the raw and earthy look of the packaging.

Ecovative aims to reduce dependency on harmful petrochemical-based plastics through the use of agricultural by-products and mushroom mycelium. By harnessing the power of nature and eliminating the pollution generated across the petroleum-based plastics supply chain, the company envisions a future where materials are not drilled, pumped and refined, but instead are grown.

Link
Lars Beller Fjetland

Discarded leather

www.beller.no

While visiting a tannery outside Bergen in Norway, Lars Beller Fjetland was struck by seeing pile after pile of discarded leather, thrown away because it did not meet the demands of perfection required by luxury brands. Any slight discolouration, insect bites or other scarring was enough for the hides to be considered unusable. The designer's frustration with this situation went on to inspire his Link series, a range of luxury products created exclusively from scrapped leather.

An intuitive linking technique allows the unlimited joining of pre-cut leather scraps to create a range of products — from pillows and beanbags to daybeds and lounge chairs. The resulting material is strong, versatile and ventilated, offering a distinctive and sophisticated solution to waste reduction.

For more on Lars Beller Fjetland, see the Q&A on page 22.

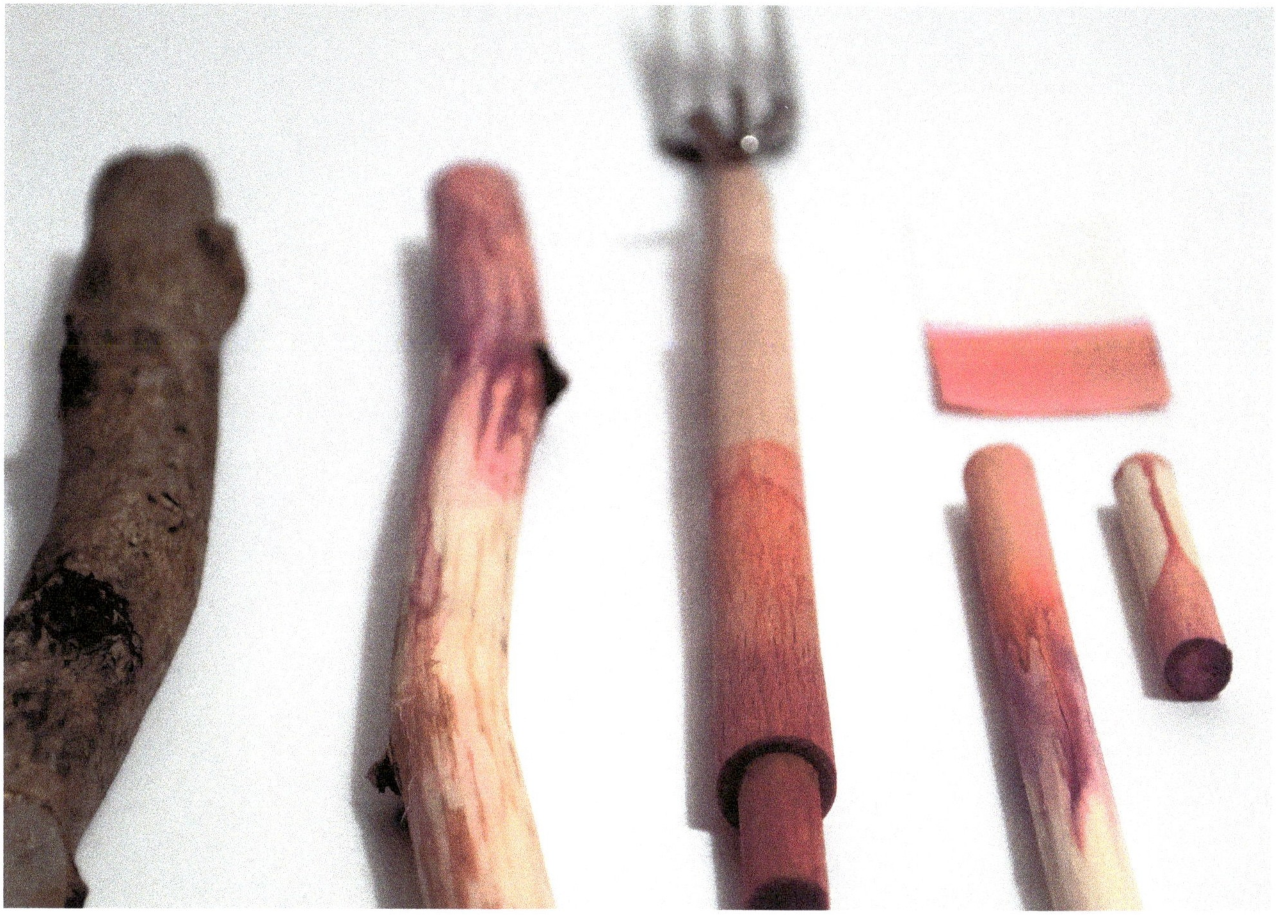

Botanic Color Collection
Elodie Gobin

Fruit and vegetables

elodiegobin.fr

Elodie Gobin's Botanic Color Collection is an ongoing research project, aimed at developing organic dyes and natural colour processes. The objective is to produce a small series of objects without consuming any raw materials, and to think about the colours of the future. The study has created ecological dyes for eco-materials, using fruit and vegetables rejected by the food industry. The most recent collection employs dyes extracted exclusively from beetroot and red cabbage.

Gobi's colours are dependent on the seasonal availability of her pigment sources – a cycle she believes consumers could become unconciously reconnected with simply by adopting 100 per cent natural colours.

Q&A: Lars Beller Fjetland

Lars Beller Fjetland grew up in Randaberg, a small town on the southwest coast of Norway – the perfect place for him to explore nature and nurture his fascination for materials. His grandfather introduced him as a child to woodwork, a passion he rediscovered in my early twenties, leaving business school to study at the Bergen Academy of Art and Design. Now he has his own studio where he designs objects with classic lines that offer functional solutions.

www.beller.no

The leather offcuts used to create the Link series were previously considered waste. The way the pieces are joined allows a wide range of products to be made – from small pillows to large carpets.

How would you describe your style?
I believe that the words 'timeless, honest and sustainable'
summarize my style. I strive to design objects that can
survive several generations. It's not just about creating
something that is rough and rugged – it's just as much
about creating classic lines that will appeal to generations
to come. I begin by stripping everything down to its
bare essentials, creating honest design, where you can
see both how and why the materials are interacting and
working together. I strive to create something that people
instantly want to interact with. It's hard to explain exactly
what causes this reaction, but I believe the effect can
be achieved by combining the right shape with the right
material. The importance of a tactile experience is highly
underestimated. I resent cheap gimmicks and aim for a
pure simplistic marriage between function and beauty.

In what way is your work sustainable?
I'm starting to see a sort of pattern in the projects that
I'm working on, as my processes are very often material
driven and angled towards alternative ways of thinking
sustainable design. Designing objects through the
use of classic lines and functional solutions is perhaps
one of the best ways of practicing sustainable design.
An object needs to endure the test of time not only
on a physical level but also on an aesthetic level. It needs
to appeal to future generations, and it is therefore
important operate on a higher level than fast fashion
and ever-changing trends.

Some of my projects are directly linked to the use
of waste materials: wood scraps (Re-turned, see page
213), discarded leather hides (Link, see page 20) and
driftwood (Drifted, see page 61).

What materials and techniques do you use?
Wood is one of the materials that I am really passionate
about. It was the first material I ever got to work with, and
it therefore represents the very root of my ever-growing
passion for designing and creating objects. Wood is an
extremely versatile material, fitting an almost unbelievable
range of purposes only limited by your own imagination.
I've have also been working with leather, marble, glass
and last but not least cork. A friend of mine introduced
me to cork, and I immediately fell in love with it. It is
squeezable, elastic, floating, waterproof, light, sound
absorbing, anti-allergenic, anti-bacterial and very
resistant. It's biodegradable and recyclable. It is warm
and soft, asking to be touched. It is the perfect material,
provided and manufactured by Mother Nature.

Woodturning is one of the techniques that I keep on
revisiting. It gives me a sensation of complete peace
of mind. It can be an extremely liberating process, where
you are sort of creating as you go. New shapes and lines
arise from the slightest interaction between the wood
and the tool.

**Have you noticed any particular trends in
sustainable design?**
I am not a particular big fan of the word 'trend', as
I personally feel that it's more related to consumerism
than to design. What I do appreciate is a greater focus
amongst designers on the idea of designing a product's
entire lifecycle, instead of just the object itself. I also
believe that we are going to see a greater shift in the
way we perceive and make use of waste.

What do you think we'll be seeing more of in the future?
I believe consumers are becoming more interested in
knowing more about the products they buy. It's not just
about how they are made, but also why.

What inspires you?
I find a lot of my inspiration through my obsession
with materials and the need to know how things work.
I have a great passion for craft, whether it's fine furniture
carpentry or metal work. I love watching old master
craftsmen in action. It's both humbling and extremely
inspirational.

Nature will always play an important role in my projects.
It is the ultimate masterpiece and a bottomless sea
of inspiration. Nature has found solutions for all of its
challenges, and they are all perfected to the smallest
of details. This inspiration drives me to work even harder
towards finding the optimal and one true solution to
my own challenges.

BioElectric
Jeongwon Ji

Bio-plastic

www.jeongwonji.com

BioElectric is a project by Jeongwon Ji that aims to challenge the archetypes of electronics through material exploration. Questioning the process that has led to manufactured products becoming smooth and streamlined, BioElectric offers an alternative approach where casings for electronic products are allowed to be expressive and encourage tactile pleasure.

Ji's solution is a bio-plastic she calls Crustic, made from the shells of Chinese mitten crabs. An alien species – now also establishing itself in British rivers – the mitten crab is an unwanted presence, but it could be seen as a useful local resource.

Through a process of trial and error in her workshop, Ji combined a small amount of red agile and glycerin with chitin polymers extracted from crushed crab shells and perfected a chemical-free 'slow production' method to make her bio-plastic. Although production time is longer, due to the use of water in place of chemicals, this non-toxic process could improve the work life of those who manufacture our electronics.

NewspaperWood
Mieke Meijer with Vij5

Newspaper

www.vij5.nl

Every day, enormous piles of newspapers are discarded and recycled into new paper. Under normal circumstances these papers do not come out of the recycling cycle again, but stay as paper. However, during her studies at the Design Academy Eindhoven in 2003, Mieke Meijer thought it would be interesting to reverse this process and turn paper into wood again, creating a new material called NewspaperWood.

The material can be cut, milled and sanded, and generally treated like any other type of wood. When a NewspaperWood log is cut, the layers of paper appear like lines of wood grain, mimicking the aesthetic of real wood.

The material is free of solvents and plasticizers, making it easy to recycle. This not only allows the option of putting sawing and sandpapering waste back into the cycle, but also taking NewspaperWood products to the scrapyard for recycling.

NewspaperWood is not intended to be a large-scale alternative to wood, but rather to promote upcycling — demonstrating how a surplus of material can be changed into something more valuable by using it in a different context.

Mini Moderns
Environmentally
Responsible Paint
Mini Moderns

Recycled paint

www.minimoderns.com

All products in the Mini Moderns Environmentally Responsible Paint range contain up to 90 per cent recycled content, made up from waste paint that has been diverted from landfill or incineration to create a premium-grade emulsion with high opacity.

One key innovation in the range is the introduction of Mini Moderns Project Pots. At 250 ml (8 oz) these pots are at least twice the size of a regular sample pot, so they can be used to complete a project, such as painting a small item of furniture, without having to buy a full-size tin.

Mini Moderns operates a predominantly 'Made in the UK' policy, which helps keep the company's carbon footprint to a minimum and supports local businesses.

Moss Story
Pia Design
(Pia Wüstenberg)

Moss

www.piadesign.eu

Considering what qualities a living organism can bring to an otherwise inanimate object, Pia Wüstenberg has undertaken an ongoing research project into the often overlooked world of moss.

Called Moss Story, the project has involved collecting samples and documenting moss growth to understand the needs of the plant well enough to use it as a material for objects. Her research has led to meeting with some leading British bryologists and exploring the ancient archives of the National History Museum, London, where centuries-old samples can still be brought back to life. One of her first experiments, Strange Vase, was made from concrete reinforced with paper, elivened by strips of moss in vertical grooves. The piece was inspired by the urban environment and Wüstenberg's admiration for 'the resilience and beauty of this family of plants that manages to infiltrate any inhabitable ground – whether urban or rural'.

Another investigation, Garden Rug, attempts to find 'new ground for organic matter within the home' and uses alpaca and merino wool as a base for a miniature moss landscape.

Botanica
Studio Formafantasma

Various materials

www.formafantasma.com

The Botanica project was commissioned by Plart, an Italian foundation concerned with the conservation of works of art and design produced in plastic.

Undertaking this project almost as historians, Studio Formafantasma investigated the pre-Bakelite period, discovering unexpected technical possibilities offered by natural polymers extracted from plants or animal derivatives. Their research led them back into the eighteenth and nineteenth centuries, when scientists began draining plants and animals to create plastics. The objects in the resulting Botanica collection are designed as if today's oil-based era had never taken place, employing materials such as rosin, dammar, copal (a sub-fossil state of amber), natural rubber, shellac and bois durci (a material composed of wood dust and animal blood).

This project aspires to offer a new perspective on plasticity, reinterpreting centuries-old technology lost in the whirl of mass production to deliver a body of work with a contemporary twist.

Plastic Fantastic
Supercyclers
(Sarah King &
Liane Rossler)

Plastic bags

supercyclers.com
www.19greekstreet.com

The Plastic Fantastic series is the result of Supercyclers designers Sarah King and Liane Rossler setting themselves the task of creating beautiful, usable vessels out of the ubiquitous supermarket plastic bag.

Created by laying the bags over existing objects and heating them until they take on new shapes, this delicate collection is intended to provoke design and development, rather than being intended for practical use.

King believes plastic 'should be as valuable as gold because it's a clever product that can last forever', and the material plays a key part in the Supercyclers' ambitions for transforming perceptions of waste materials through the design of products and furniture.

N.I.P.S.
Usedesign

Flour, salt, water, natural resin

www.usedesign.it

N.I.P.S. is a conceptual project by Italian studio Usedesign that creates kitchen vessels out of dough made from stale bread and salt. Playing with notions of the uselessness of the useful and the usefulness of the useless, the project mixes waste food with natural resins, transforming it into practical objects.

The designers champion these simple, natural ingredients, capable of forming easily malleable doughs with a strong structural resistance, and characterized by a refined and natural texture.

Bio Composite
Mugi Yamamoto

Earth

www.mugiyamamoto.com

Bio Composite is the result of Mugi Yamamoto's research into making new materials from the loam-rich soil of Switzerland. Intent on keeping the products as eco-friendly and recyclable as possible, Yamamoto resolved to use only biodegradable materials and not to fire them, trying out 55 varying combinations with 24 different ingredients.

Each sample was pressed into the same mould and then air-dried before testing. Many performed surprisingly well and could serve as a seat for a stool only 2 cm (5 in) thick, yet strong enough to support a person's weight. Yamamoto believes he has discovered a 'new and fascinating material' that is 'very cheap, easy to make, accessible to everyone, ecological and very resilient.'

A4ADesign · Paul Anderson · Arrowhead · Atelier Volvox · Maarten Baas · Nick Barberton · Bernardita Marambio Design Studio · Blakebrough + King · Bror Boije · Kennedy Brown · James Carroll · Chiaozza · Brent Comber · Company · Sebastian Cox · Reinier de Jong · Design Soil · DesignByThem · Piet Hein Eek · Karin Ekwall · Emeco · Lars Beller Fjetland · Ryan Frank · Joost Gehem · Geoffrey Fisher Design · Natanel Gluska · Emiliano Godoy · Gompf + Kehrer · Grain · Breg Hanssen · Philip Henderson · Hettler Tüllmann · Merel Karhof · Xerock Kim · La Quercia 21 · Lasfera · Loll Designs · Mater · Gareth Neal & Kevin Gauld · Rentaro Nishimura and Mango Club · Odd Matter · Oxgut Hose Co. · RaFa-kids · Yoav Reches · Rekindle · Magnus Scholz · Stephen Shaheen · Springtime · Philippe Starck · Studio Aisslinger · Studio Libertíny · Studio NOCC · Leonardo Talarico · Nina Tolstrup · Mark Tuckey · Lucy Turner · Tyanjane Club · Marjan van Aubel & Jamie Shaw · Kirstie van Noort & Rogier Arients · VE2 · Volk · Katie Walker · Maria Westerberg · Debbie Wijskamp

Furniture

Havearest
A4Adesign
(Giovanni Rivolta, Nicoletta Savioni & Markús Stefánsson)

Cardboard
Armchair, H: 80 cm (31½ in), W: 100 cm, D: 80 cm (31½ in)

www.a4adesign.it

The Havearest series of armchairs and two-seater sofas are assembled from cardboard and water-based glue. Havearest is surprisingly strong and is aimed at the retail, events and contract sectors because it comes into its own in large spaces that make the most of its geometric silhouette and scenographic potential.

All of A4Adesign's products are made from 100 per cent recycled and recyclable honeycomb cardboard, chosen not only for its eco credentials but also because it is strong, lightweight and offers great value for money. The finished product costs less than similar products made from other materials, and the entire manufacturing process is better value, from assembly, which requires no specific skills, to eventual disposal.

For more on A4Adesign, see the Q&A on page 36.

Chaise for the Unphased
Paul Anderson

Reclaimed oak

www.paulandersonart.co.uk

Chaise for the Unphased is typical of Paul Anderson's highly distinctive, elemental furniture. Driven by a love of discarded materials, Anderson sources relic oak from defunct barn roofs, boats, gates and fences to create sculptural but functional designs in his workshop near the wild Atlantic coast of Devon, England.

Assembled without the use of power tools and using simple mortice-and-tenon joints, the timbers are always left unplaned to better communicate their character and history. As Anderson admits, 'I use a mixture of instinct and only very elementary techniques; my tools are a shambles; for me it is all materials, then design.'

Q&A: A4Adesign

A4Adesign, run by architects Nicoletta Savioni and Giovanni Rivolta, is based in Milan and, since 2002, has been involved in the creation and production of stage settings, installations, furniture and toys in recycled, recyclable and reusable honeycomb cardboard.

www.a4adesign.it

Bookstack shelving made of honeycomb cardboard is light, sturdy, stackable and flame retardant.

In what way is your work sustainable?
At A4Adesign, sustainability is considered an essential value and also an inspiring principle, a fait accompli and a constant commitment.

Our motto 'giochiamo pulito' (we play clean/let's play clean) expresses this idea, but it is also an invitation to people, groups and companies to choose this option and work together to develop useful projects that are consistent with sustainable development. The motto also underscores our creative, project-based and playful approach to work.

How would you describe your style?
Design is the poetry of objects; it means interpreting and communicating many things.

In our company, design is versatile, simple, with linear forms and an evocative touch. Sometimes it is über-decorative, it often has a dream-like quality, and incorporates playful things and forms inspired by fantasy and by the world of children.

When necessary, our designs call on contrasts, alternating curvaceous and sinuous shapes with rigorous essential forms, and we are able to use our sensitivity and our capacity to fine-tune our skills.

What materials and techniques do you use?
Honeycomb cardboard looks simple but it is terribly complicated. In order to use it, you have to know it inside out. Having worked with cardboard for many years, we know its qualities and its limits, the methods and techniques for using it, the applications and the graphics. It means asking the material to stretch itself, especially when it is used in nontraditional situations, knowing exactly how it will behave and how the project has to be.

What are you working on at the moment and what would you like to work on in the future?
Currently we are working on urban-scale projects such as EXPO suite – a set of modules that can be combined in different ways to create custom-made furniture – and we would like in the future to develop this kind of project that involved people.

Have you noticed any particular trends in sustainable design?
I would say a kind of new honesty in showing materials and also pervasive research into using new ones.

What materials or techniques do you think we'll be seeing more of in the future?
Any materials that are competitive from many points of view will be used, but sustainability will be more and more an essential value.

Cardboard furniture, toys and animals are easy to transport and assemble for special events.

Harris Swing
Arrowhead

Fallen timber, rope
W (top): 95 cm (37¼ in), W (base): 142 cm (56 in)

arrowhead-nc.com

Arrowhead is a two-man craft operation located in North Carolina. Sustainability is built into their business model from the ground up. All their timber is sourced from a local sawmill that specializes in wood that has fallen naturally, which means that the wood used for each piece is unique and variable, depending on what is available. The workshop also tries to be a no-waste shop. Scraps from one project are turned into another, and unusable wood scrap is converted to charcoal.

Arrowhead designed the Harris Swing, which comes in one- or two-person options, to be built entirely without fasteners. Local North Carolina timber and rope are the only two materials used to hold this swing together.

For more on Arrowhead, see the Q&A on page 40.

Re-Mix
Atelier Volvox (Lea Gerber & Sophie Liechti)

Salvaged wood
H: 50 cm (19⅝ in), W: 52–56 cm (20½–22 in), D: 24 cm (9½ in)

www.ateliervolvox.ch

Re-Mix is a verstile shelving system by Atelier Volvox, assembled from scrap wood panels. The material is provided by the short sections of waste material inevitably produced in carpentry workshops when planks are sawn to shorter lengths. Although these pieces are usually too short to be of any use, the Re-Mix system turns this to its advantage; each part becomes a single modular unit so that a storage area can be built up shelf by shelf.

An edge or two of each piece is finished in colourful, non-toxic paint, providing a friendly contrast with the bare finish of the pine or chipboard panels.

Q&A: Arrowhead

Arrowhead is a small workshop in Raleigh, North Carolina, that designs and constructs furniture, art and structures using metal, wood and leather with a focus on craftsmanship and natural materials.

www.arrowhead-nc.com

Arrowhead's Trestle Base Dining Table is made of locally sourced quarter-sawn red oak and steel.

How did you get involved in furniture design?
I've never considered myself a designer. I'm a builder,
a maker. I was always into DIY culture and letting
available materials dictate design. I was a farmer
for several years, and grew accustomed to and proficient
at building little contraptions, structures and fixes on the
fly for very specific purposes and with virtually no budget.
My design aesthetic evolved as I grew more comfortable
with materials and tools. I worked in a cabinet shop
during slow winters and learned from incredible
craftspeople, and I spent a couple of years working on
historic houses for a local contractor. The exposure to
several centuries of different techniques and materials
afforded me an understanding of structures and forms
that I employ in everything I build. I believe in the beauty
of structure and function. I'm routinely blown away
by the vastness of incredible, locally available materials.

How would you describe your style?
Modern. Industrial. Southern. (Hopefully) timeless.
Accessible. Humble.

What materials and techniques do you use?
Locally available lumber from an independent, owner-
operated mill. Industrial steel. We use modern tools
and techniques. All visible welds are tig welded — a
process that requires more time and expense but which
is stronger and inherently better looking. We attempt
to combine several materials in each of our pieces.
In doing so, we attempt to incorporate one material into
the other, rather than, say, slapping a piece of wood on
a steel base. We avoid fasteners when possible.
We countersink steel in wood and wood into steel, leather
in wood, etc. We attempt to use one material to celebrate
another. We deal in contrast and complements rather
than aggregations of individual components.

What inspires you?
I'm inspired by materials, by spaces, and by the creative
ideas of people who don't even know they're 'designing'.
I like making people happy. I look up to the makers I've
worked for, and everyone out there making it on their
own. I'm energized by collaboration and creative
synergies. I believe that the best talent is hidden in old
barns and garages housing humble craftspeople building
what they want and need with love.

What are you working on at the moment?
I'm most excited about converting a good friend's
tobacco barn into her writing studio. I'm also looking
forward to developing a line of seating based on a
notebook of ideas we've been developing for a long
time. We're also working on collaborating with makers
working in totally different media – a denim company,
a motorcycle brand, a chocolate company.

We're hoping to position ourselves to design and build
whole spaces as we mature as a company. It's difficult to
maximize our aesthetic impact by building single pieces.
We don't want our work to dominate, but we make very
recognizable statements when given the opportunity.

**Have you noticed any particular trends
in sustainable design?**
To be honest, I don't spend a ton of time following design
trends. Seems like I'm noticing a surge in well-built
modular design and an interest in smaller spaces. I love
both. People are increasingly mobile, and our generation
seems much more interested in smaller, nicer spaces.
We love the idea of building pieces that folks can carry
with them forever. Function-as-form seems to be on the
upswing, too. We try to make bold the processes that
made the piece, and it seems there is increasingly
a market for that.

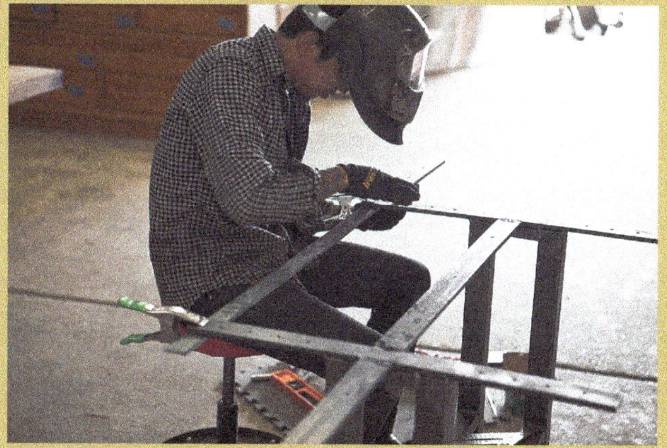

All Arrowhead designs are
developed and constructed
in-house, with a close focus
on craftsmanship.

Steel Plated
Maarten Baas

Recycled steel
Various sizes

www.maartenbaas.com

Steel Plated is a collection of recycled-steel patchwork furniture by Dutch designer Maarten Baas. Selecting scrap cars to make palettes of green, blue, red, gold and grey, Baas cut bonnets, doors and roofs into small, irregularly shaped steel plates and welds them together one by one, creating a glossy, mosaic-like effect.

The furniture incorporates further scrap elements, such as a battery-charged light built into a coffee table. The controls of the floor light utilize a swivel arm, while a pop-up bonnet door was built to hide an extra seat and drinks cabinet. Although heavy, the pieces can be wheeled into their desired location.

Captain's Chair
Nick Barberton

Fallen walnut
H: 82 cm (32¼ in), W: 78 cm (30¾ in), D: 75 cm (29½ in)

www.nickbarberton.co.uk

Working exclusively in sustainable British hardwoods – often from fallen trees – Nick Barberton enjoys bridging the world between art and craft, and attempts to best display the character and essence of each piece of wood.

The Captain's Chair was made from a walnut tree that fell at Manor Farm in Dorset, England. Barberton had it cut into planks and created this piece of sinuous, elegant furniture, fabricating the laminated backrest and carving a pattern on the seat. The legs were jointed using a method developed by the legendary Californian woodworker Sam Maloof.

The Reliving Room
Bernardita Marambio
Design Studio

Mañío wood, Demodé
Various sizes

www.bernarditamarambio.cl

The Reliving Room is a collection of furniture created using structures made out of mañío wood, supporting panels of Demodé. Demodé is a new material cladding, made from waste textiles – salvaged from factories in Santiago, Chile – which are torn up and then pressed into sheets. The fabric is held together with biodegradable adhesive and modified starch to give structural strength, while revealing all the different colours, textures and threads of the component materials. Demodé aims to be a simple means of allowing materials once created for a product with a limited life cycle to be given a more permanent purpose.

Natural Grain Kite Stool
Blakebrough + King

Wheat or rice straw
H: 39 cm (15⅜ in), W: 30 cm (11¾ in), D: 30 cm (11¾ in)

blakebroughking.com
www.19greekstreet.com

The Natural Grain Kite Stool uses the form of Blakebrough + King's own classic aluminium Kite Stool as a mould. The mould is stuffed with food by-products – wheat straw or rice straw – and is then compressed in a 2-tonne press to form a biodegradable chair or side table whose graphic form contains its original composition.

This innovative process could be used with any material to create a new stool or side table out of waste.

BlockChair
Bror Boije for
Green Furniture Sweden

Mixed FSC-certified wood
H: 81cm (31⅞in), W: 41.5cm (16⅜in), D: 47.8cm (18⅞in)

greenfurniture.se

Green Furniture's BlockChair is made from recycled timber scraps sourced from Kährs, the Swedish wooden-floor manufacturer. The chair consists mainly of FSC-certified Swedish oak, assembled in the traditional way using bone glue. It is then treated with all-natural, solvent-free oils, which protect and preserve its sturdy, no-nonsense design.

Conceived by Bror Boije, one of Sweden's all-time best-selling furniture designers, Green Furniture believe the BlockChair may be the most sustainable all-natural restaurant/conference chair in the world – to the point that they declare, 'You could eat it if only it wasn't so hard to chew.'

Embrace
Kennedy Brown

Reclaimed calophyllum timber, stainless steel, Corian
H: 43 cm (16⅞ in), L: 76 cm (29⅞ in), W: 28.8 cm (11⅜ in)

www.kennedybrown.co.nz

Throughout his work, designer Kennedy Brown seeks to express his Pacific homeland, Aotearoa (New Zealand), drawing inspiration from culture, both old and new, on his doorstep.

Embrace is a contemporary single-seater bench that explores and combines Westernized and Polynesian structures and fabrication techniques with modern materials and processes. Embrace was designed to utilize smaller offcuts of timber from the building industry, and has been made in native kauri, tawa and calophyllum. The bench has also been made from a recycled calophyllum shipping pallet, incorporating nail holes, bumps and knots, providing character while relating the story of its previous existence.

Three-Legged Stool
James Carroll for Makers & Brothers

Birch, ash, water-based wood stain
H: 38 cm (15 in), W: 25 cm (9⅞ in), D: 20 cm (7⅞ in)

www.makersandbrothers.com

A classically shaped stool with three legs and a wonderfully gouged top surface, the Three-Legged Stool is created by James Carroll for Makers & Brothers, using locally sourced birch and ash.

Available in both coloured and non-coloured versions, the stool is a simple piece, inspired by traditional furniture shapes. The legs are coloured naturally, using water-based wood stain in shades of blue, green, pink, red and black. The top is finished using a gouge chisel, which is used to gently texture the surface with small hollows and dimples.

Carroll sees the potential beauty in each piece of timber he picks up. He then works with the natural features of each piece, never creating the same object twice. As a result, subtle yet beautiful variations exist between each stool.

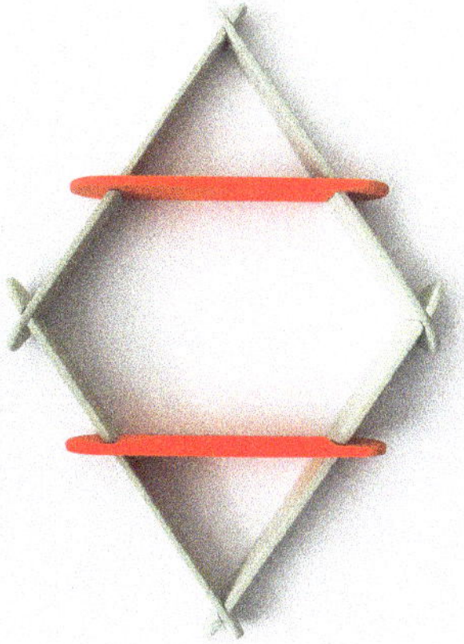

A-Frames
Chiaozza (Terri Chiao & Adam Frezza)

Wood
Various sizes

chiaozza.eternitystew.com

Chiaozza's A-Frames is a series of wall pieces experimenting with interlocking wooden joinery, geometric forms and bright colour combinations. The pieces are hung on a nail and can be displayed as aesthetic ornaments themselves, or used for displaying arrangements of small objects.

Inspired by a Danish folk design from the island of Amager, near Copenhagen, each A-Frame uses lengths of sustainable American hardwoods, hand-cut with traditional woodworking saws and assembled using simple wooden lap joints with no adhesive. They are finished in non-toxic matt acrylic paints and various wood stains.

T-Cup
Brent Comber

Wood
H: 40.6 cm (16 in), Diam.: 31.8 cm (12½ in)

www.brentcomber.com

The round, flat surface of the T-Cup charts the life of a tree by displaying its growth rings and unique grain pattern.

The inspiration behind the T-Cup came from Eva Zeisel's ceramic tea sets. Zeisel, a Hungarian-born American industrial designer, is renowned for her exquisite glass and ceramic objects based on geometric shapes. The sensuous forms of her pieces represent the natural, organic curves of the human body, as does each piece in the T-Cup series.

Canadian designer Brent Comber works with reclaimed wood from trees cut down in schoolyards, parks or residences, often because of a damaged root structure. As a result, the wood used in each T-Cup varies.

Stool and Shoes
Company (Johan Olin & Aamu Song) with Editions in Craft

Straw, wool, wood
Stool, H: 45 cm (17¾ in), Diam.: 35 cm (13¾ in)
Shoes, H: 12 cm (4¾ in), L: 27 cm (10⅝ in), W: 15 cm (5⅞ in)

www.com-pa-ny.com
www.editionsincraft.com

The 2012 Farmer's Gold workshop held in Dalsland, the centre of Swedish straw craft, was designed to bring together European designers and local artisans to celebrate and promote straw craft (see page 229).

Through an exchange of ideas and techniques, the designers and artisans explored the material and created new products designed to 'challenge the traditional distinctions between design and craft'.

This set of stool and shoes were developed by the design brand Company, who were invited to attend by the event's organizers, Editions in Craft.

Suent Superlight Chair
Sebastian Cox

Coppiced hazel
H: 74 cm (29⅛ in), W: 37 cm (14⅝ in), D: 46 cm (18⅛ in),

sebastiancox.co.uk

This lightweight chair is made from coppiced hazel, an abundant and sustainable wood, harvested by hand in Kent, England. Its back legs are steam-bent to give a strong construction, while the colours are achieved using a natural dye made from vinegar and rusty nails.

Coppicing is an ancient method of woodland management where trees are cut just above ground level. Harvestable, straight-growing 'rods' re-sprout vigorously from the stump, providing the next crop of wood. The process is repeated every seven years or so to give a sustainable crop of usable wood. Managed correctly in this way, this resource is inexhaustible.

Sebastian Cox is an award-winning designer based in London whose work is inherently sustainable. He manufactures his pieces by hand, and therefore has a deep understanding of, and engagement with, his materials. This largely informs the designs, which are developed at the workbench rather than at a drawing board or on a CAD program.

For more on Sebastian Cox, see the Q&A on page 128.

Steel Chair
Reinier de Jong

Recycled and sustainably sourced wood
H: 77 cm (30¼ in), W: 46 cm (18⅛ in), D: 47 cm (18½ in)

www.reinierdejong.com

Reinier de Jong's Steel Chairs are made from the wooden handles of humble tools and objects such as brooms, rakes, spades and flagpoles. Each item betrays traces of its former use through its unique patina, revealing the effects of soil, rain, hands, air and sunlight. Steel is intended to be a modest chair, reflecting the everyday nature of its original components.

Incorporating different types of salvaged wood, the chairs also make use of sustainable ash from FSC-certified sources, finished with non-toxic paint. The new wood is then notched in places to reveal the grain beneath, marrying both types of wood.

Butter Stool
DesignByThem
(Nicholas Karlovasitis & Sarah Gibson)

100% recycled plastic (HDPE)
H: 44.1 cm (17⅜ in), W: 38 cm (15 in), D: 40 cm (15¾ in)

www.designbythem.com

The Butter range is created from 100 per cent recycled content, derived almost entirely from post-consumer recycled milk containers. Suitable for indoor and outdoor use, the robustness of the pieces, combined with their textured surface, ensures a long product life. The products' ability to be shipped as flat pieces also reduces their environmental impact during distribution.

DesignByThem also offer a product stewardship programme, taking in products to be repaired, reused or recycled. The company believes that good design makes our lives more enjoyable and appreciative of our environment, and that design education is crucial for creating a more innovative and sustainable society.

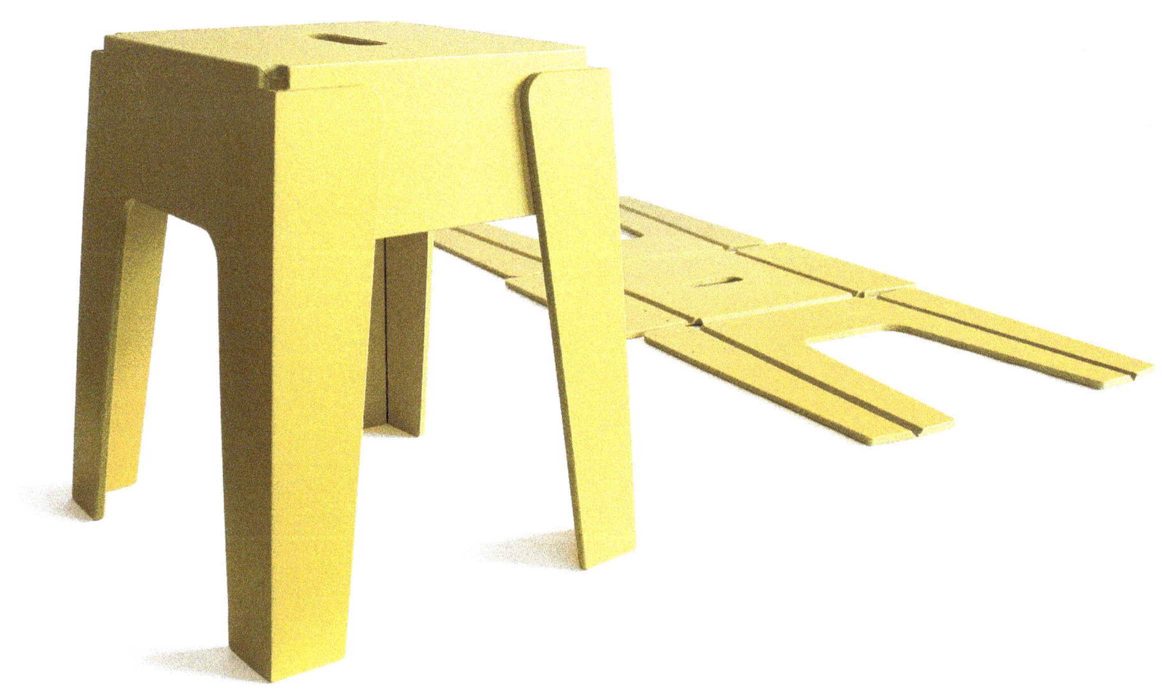

Outside In
Design Soil (Rie Asaka)

White ash, plywood, cardboard
H: 73.5 cm (29 in), W: 128.4 cm (50½ in), D: 60 cm (23⅝ in)

www.designsoil.jp

Addressing the paradox that cardboard packaging has a short useful lifespan compared to its durability, Rie Asaka's Outside In desk attempts to give new life to waste packing materials, discarded once they have fulfilled their original purpose.

During shipping, the hollow plywood tabletop is used to contain the legs of the desk. However, after assembly, the strips of cardboard packaging are inserted between the two thin sheets of plywood, providing rigid support to the otherwise flexible surfaces.

By using the packaging cardboard as the core, the Outside In desk provides a neat and completely integrated, waste-free product.

Waste Waste 40x40
Piet Hein Eek

Scrapwood
Various sizes

www.pietheineek.nl

Piet Hein Eek's Waste Waste 40x40 project came into existence as a reaction to the annoyance of having to throw away material because it was too expensive to do anything with it – not because it was worthless but because the cost of labour was too high. Eek realized that if waste timber was uniformly processed into 40 mm (1⅝ in) cubes it would become an efficient construction material, and make use of even the smallest offcuts.

Although the cubes are used to construct only an outer skin, the uniform size and straight edges nevertheless define the appearance of the products made from it.

For more on Piet Hein Eek, see the Q&A on page 58.

Åsta and Friends
Karin Ekwall

Wood
Various sizes

www.karinekwall.no

Designer Karin Ekwall created the Åsta series of collapsible furniture as part of her degree collection. The table, bench and stool are made entirely of locally sourced sustainable wood and contain no glue or fixings. The pieces are very easy to assemble and disassemble without screws, nails or additional tools, and because they are simple to flat-pack, they can be transported with a minimum of energy. The furniture is based on traditional, Scandinavian carpentry, and is all made by hand.

Q&A: Piet Hein Eek

As a boy, Piet Hein Eek was always making things. After studying at the Design Academy Eindhoven in the Netherlands, he became an industrial designer, but has maintained his love of making things. No longer purely a designer, Piet now also produces, distributes and sells his products through his company. He also works on private commissions and limited-edition projects.

www.pietheineek.nl

Piet Hein Eek's Waste collection is created from scraps of reclaimed wood and finished in high-gloss water-based lacquer.

How would you describe your style?

I hope I don't have a style. I'm inspired by materials, technique and craftsmanship – these generate new ideas for each project. The products may not be visually similar, but they are family because they're all made with the same attitude.

In what way is your work sustainable?

The most important issue is that they're not thrown away. Because my products are inspired by the specific quality of the materials they are made of, I design them in such a way to celebrate this quality – they often age in a beautiful way, extending their life. Also because of the respect for material, I always try to be as efficient as possible: the products are produced trying not to waste material and energy.

What materials and techniques do you use?

We have a big metal, wood and ceramic workshop, and also an upholstery, so I use any materials, techniques and machines that we have or that are close to me.

What are you working on at the moment, and what do you hope to work on in the future?

We're always working on products for the collection. At the moment, the Waste Waste 40x40 project (see page 56) is very nice, and we are also working on also the biggest ceramic vase we can make. At the opposite end of this spectrum of extravagant products, we're making the Crisis 2013 series of cupboards and the Fat Ceramics range (see page 205). Apart from that, I'm working on a project setting the ultimate step in creating the biggest difference between rubbish and value. We're going to make busts from our own garbage from the home, the workplace and holidays. If it works, Waste Bust will probably be the final conclusion of the Nature and Scrap project, in which I designed products using natural and waste materials, and turned the world upside down by acting as if labour is free and materials are worth a fortune.

Have you noticed any particular trends in sustainable design?

The things that are trendy are mainly focused on the communication of a trend. To be efficient with energy and materials isn't a trend but a necessity.

What materials or techniques do you think we'll be seeing more of in the future?

I don't think there will a specific change in the materials used by designers, but some of the materials often used now will perhaps become scare and therefore very exclusive in the future. In general, I think materials will be more expensive because of scarceness.

The Crisis 2013 Cabinet is part of Piet Hein Eek's experimental Crisis range, which is constructed almost entirely from plywood sheeting.

111 Navy Chair
Emeco with Coca-Cola

65% recycled PET, 35% glass fibre
H: 86 cm (33⅞ in), W: 39 cm (15⅜ in), D: 50 cm (19⅝ in)

www.emeco.net

Looking for a way to keep their bottles out of landfill and upcycle them into an iconic structural item, Coca-Cola initiated a collaboration with chair manufacturer Emeco, hoping to address this environmental problem. Emeco responded by creating a plastic version of its iconic 1006 Navy Chair, using this recycled PET plastic to build a tough, one-piece, scratch-resistant design, suitable for heavy-duty use.

The new chair takes its name from the 111 bottles used for its manufacture. Over the course of its production, the 111 Navy Chair is expected to keep 3 million plastic Coke bottles out of landfill each year.

Drifted
Lars Beller Fjetland
for Discipline

Ash, cork
Barstool, H: 75 cm (29½ in), Diam. (seat): 33 cm (13 in)
Chair, H: 85 cm (33½ in), L: 46 cm (18⅛ in), W: 51 cm (20⅛ in)
Stool, H: 45 cm (17¾ in), Diam. (seat): 33 cm (13 in)

www.beller.no
www.discipline.eu

The inspiration for the Drifted series came from a visit to Øygarden, outside Bergen, on the coast of Norway. While walking along the water's edge, designer Lars Beller Fjetland became aware of the varied materials and objects that had floated ashore. Driftwood had been bleached and scoured by the ocean, old cork had been ground into unrecognizable shapes. These textures, shapes and materials established the basis of Drifted, a set of two stools and a chair. The name plays off the materials' ability to drift with the waves.

The series is constructed from sustainably sourced ash and cork. The fusion of these two materials creates a set of functional, and comfortable, seats.

For more on Lars Beller Fjetland, see the Q&A on page 22.

100% Zero
Ryan Frank

Reclaimed wood
H: 50 cm (19⅝ in), W: 50 cm (9⅝ in), D: 40 cm (15¾ in)

www.ryanfrank.net

This collection of occasional tables is the realization of designer Ryan Frank's attempts to produce furniture with no budget, completely avoiding virgin material. The tables are made from reclaimed bits of wood, such as scaffolding planks and pallets, and finished off with a selection of salvaged wheels or handles.

Frank was pleased to find a use for his growing collection of salvaged castor wheels and drawer handles. As he says, 'When salvaging, one rarely finds a complete set of wheels – usually a few are missing. So by simply adjusting the height of each table leg, I was able to use a mix of different style castor wheels to complete the table.'

Glitch
Ryan Frank

Bamboo, cork
Desk, L: 180 cm (70⅞ in), H: 120 cm (47¼ in), D: 80 cm (31½ in)
Shelf, L: 165 cm (65 in), H: 200 cm (78¾ in), D: 50 cm (19¾ in)

www.ryanfrank.net

Glitch is the debut office-furniture piece from Ryan Frank. Comprising a desk and a shelving unit, the design uses sustainable bamboo and steam-bonded Spanish cork to create a distinctive tactile workstation.

The desk has a work surface of silky smooth bamboo and an integrated cork pinboard, while the shelves have a set of chunky hooks buckled along a length of jute webbing, providing a fun and functional way of suspending a multitude of unstackable objects.

As with much of Frank's work, no glues are used, only screws, and the main materials have solid eco credentials. Bamboo soaks up greenhouse gases and converts them to new green growth without the need for petroleum-powered tractors or poisonous pesticides and fertilizers. Likewise, the sustainable cork forests of Mediterranean Europe absorb an estimated 10 million tonnes of CO_2 annually, and provide a valuable habitat for endangered species and migratory birds.

Transformation and Distribution Centre for Abandoned Household Items
Joost Gehem

Home furnishings
Various sizes

www.joostgehemdesign.com

As a consequence of the thousands of deaths, divorces and bankruptcies that occur each year, many household inventories are left without a home. Discovering that much of this ends up in the local dump, Joost Gehem was struck by the potential of this vast resource of raw materials.

His Transformation and Distribution Centre for Abandoned Household Items grinds down furniture and turns it into new products such as stools. Rather than being driven by recycling concerns, Gehem's priority is providing a more respectful way of relieving the owners of these goods, allowing the objects to live on in a product with new value. This allows him to pay the owner and not the other way around.

The Majestic
Natanel Gluska

Jarrah-wood railway sleepers
L: 400 cm (157½ in), W: 100 cm (39⅜ in)

www.natanelgluska.com

The Majestic is a fittingly named dining table, heftily constructed from 70 sections of recycled jarrah wood. Cut from obsolete railway sleepers, the timber is preserved in its original state, form and texture, creating a functional piece of art that not only respects its origins but emphasizes its beauty by showing it in a different light.

The Majestic is typical of Natanel Gluska's reputation for crafting one-off, playful, roughly hewn, artistic furniture pieces. Gluska champions the importance on the culture of design of individuals who still make by hand and exhibit a freedom of expression missing in mass-produced design.

For more on Natanel Gluska, see the Q&A on page 66.

Q&A: Natanel Gluska

Furniture designer Natanel Gluska used to be an unhappy painter who didn't really like to be alone in his studio day and night. He wanted to get out into the fresh air and use his body, so he started using chainsaws and carving chairs from logs he found in the park. Now his furniture pieces, each one unique and hewn from a single piece of wood, straddle the boundary of art and design.

www.natanelgluska.com

Using a chainsaw and hand-drawn sketches, Gluska creates unique hybrids of sculpture and functional form. Chair no 91 is made of oak.

Describe your style?
My style is diversified, very intuitive, and it depends very much on the place, the surrounding and my budget. I like to use materials that are laying around and give them a new life.

What inspires you?
Inspiration is something you have no control of. It could come from a great piece of music, a book or the shadow of a cat.

In what way is your work sustainable?
The wood I'm using is from sick or dead trees – it's a kind of recycling.

What are you currently working on?
I have recently started to cast some of my wooden pieces in bronze, and I already have three pieces that were recently shown in Dubai. I will be continuing to develop more pieces for this collection.

Since coming to Asia, I've also had the opportunity to recycle railway sleepers – namely, jarrah and ironwood — and have produced a few unique pieces including a table 4 x 1 metres (13 x 3 feet) long made of 70 pieces of recycled jarrah railway sleepers.

Have you noticed any trends in sustainable design?
I don't know about trends, but there is more and more awareness of sustainable design and architecture, for sure.

Which materials and techniques do you think we will see more of in the future?
There will be new solutions for housing in sensitive places where there are natural disasters like earthquakes, floods and storms. There will be new materials to heat, to cool and to preserve. There will also be new alternative energy systems. 3D printers will get cheaper, we will able to produce faster and there will be more custom-made products. And, of course, even faster communication.

Top: The Crocodile bench was made from recycled jarrah-wood railway sleepers.

Bottom: Chair no 14 is carved from beech. The domed seat clearly shows the cutting marks of Gluska's chainsaw.

Snowjob
Emiliano Godoy with Ecoist

Post-industrial sweet wrapper waste, post-consumer
recycled paper, stainless steel, FSC-certified maple
H: 70 cm (27⅝ in), W: 50 cm (19⅝ in), D: 50 cm (19⅝ in)

www.emilianogodoy.com
www.ecoist.com

Huge numbers of misprinted sweet wrappers are thrown away every day. Emiliano Godoy teamed up with Ecoist, a company specializing in transforming this material into women's bags, to work on a new application. They chose to develop a chair, Snowjob, which takes its name from the American expression for a cover-up story.

The chair consists of two main components. A wooden structure made from FSC-certified wood with a vegetable-based, biodegradable finish forms the legs and general support. This also partly disassembles by means of stainless steel hardware, reducing the chair's shipping size by half, and consequently reducing transportation and storage impacts.

A cover then slips over the wooden structure to form the seat, back and armrests. This is made from recovered sweet wrappers, which are cut into small pieces, folded into rectangles and joined to form large surfaces. An internal reinforcement made from post-consumer recycled paper adds rigidity and resistance.

The wooden structure is made with simple woodworking hand tools, while the cover requires only a box cutter, thus eliminating any complex or expensive tooling.

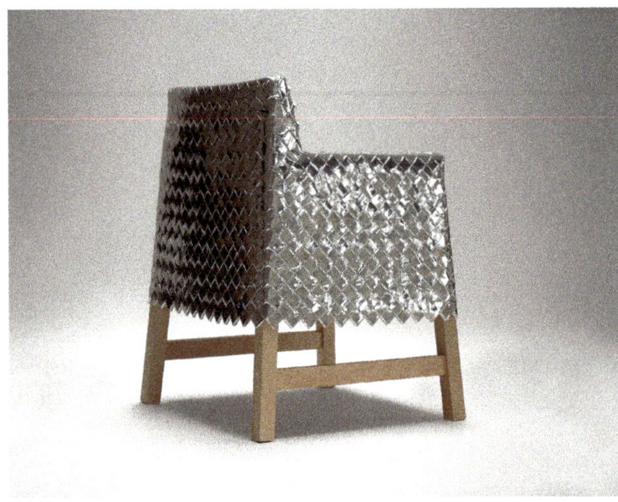

Paper Table
Gompf + Kehrer
(Verena Stella Gompf
& Cordula Kehrer)

Paper, glass
H: 40 cm (15¾ in), Diam.: 50 cm (19⅝ in)

www.gompf-kehrer.com

Paper Table resembles a stack of paper, or the profile of a large illustrated book. The table is handmade from recycled paper by a fairtrade cooperative in Vietnam. After cutting, sampling and sorting, the paper is compressed into a new material with a texture similar to wood grain.

The colours of the tables are entirely random, and dependent on the particular source of unwanted paper that is available at the time. For this reason, each table is a unique piece of sustainable design.

Dish
Grain (James &
Chelsea Minola)

FSC-certified ash
Coffee table, H: 40.6 cm (16 in), Diam.: 81.3 cm (32 in)
Side table, H: 40.6 cm (16 in), Diam.: 45.7 cm (18 in)

www.graindesign.com

Taking inspiration from hand-carved African furniture,
the Dish tables are created with help from technology.
A CNC router is used to cut away the wooden bowl,
leaving behind a slope that quickly levels to a flat surface.
Built in the USA from FSC-certified ash, Dish is available
in coffee- and side-table sizes, with a choice of clear oil
or non-toxic black stain finish.

Grain is committed to socially and environmentally
responsible design. Their work unites current
manufacturing technologies with age-old craft
techniques. As committed members of 1% For The
Planet, 1 percent of their annual revenue goes back
to environmental non-profit organizations such as
the Surfrider Foundation, Organic Seed Alliance,
PCC Farmland Trust, the Nature Conservancy and
the National Park Foundation.

Spool Wall System
Grain (James & Chelsea Minola)

Paper
Spool, W: 15.2 cm (6 in), Diam.: 8.3 cm (3¼ in)
Connector, H: 3 mm (⅛ in), Diam.: 7 cm (2¾ in)

www.graindesign.com

Spool is a build-it-yourself modular wall system that can be assembled into a variety of freestanding structures, such as screens, table bases or partitions. The main components are made from paper spools upcycled from the Los Angeles apparel industry, each of which has a colourful graphic pattern indicating the type of fibre it once held. These elements can then be assembled with connectors made of 100 per cent post-consumer waste chipboard.

Because of the versatility of the product, the Spool system can grow with the needs of the consumer, and become many different things. At the end of its useful life, it can simply be recycled locally with waste paper.

Framed
Breg Hanssen with Vij5

NewspaperWood, cardboard, steel frame
30 panels, H: 104 cm (41 in), W: 84 cm (33⅛ in), D: 42 cm (16½ in)
18 panels, H: 62 cm (24⅜ in), W: 84 cm (33⅛ in), D: 42 cm (16½ in)

www.breghanssen.nl
www.vij5.nl

Framed is a series of distinctive cupboards, designed by Breg Hanssen together with Dutch interior manufacturer Vij5. This cabinet consists of a solid steel frame, available in a range of sizes and colours, which contrasts with the distinctive 'neutral' colour of the planks that complete it.

The planks are made of NewspaperWood, a concept developed by Mieke Meijer (see page 25), where recycled newspapers are laminated together and pressed into a wood-like material. It even has a grain when cut, giving character to the panels.

NewspaperWood is made without solvents or plasticizers, so it can easily be recycled back into paper again if desired.

Treasure Chest
Philip Henderson

FSC-certified oak, Valchromat
H: 42 cm (16½ in), L: 100 cm (39⅜ in), D: 40 cm (15¾ in)

www.philiphendersonstudio.co.uk

Philip Henderson's Treasure Chest is intended to be a durable box with a timeless aesthetic, fulfilling a range of needs throughout the owner's life, from toy box to clothes storage.

The box uses panels of organically dyed Valchromat, an eco-friendly fibreboard made from forest waste, residue from timber mills and recycled pine. These are held in place with a frame of sustainable European FSC-certified oak, treated with vegetable oil and wax-based Osmo oil. Being oiled rather than lacquered makes the wood easy to sand smooth if damaged.

Likewise, the fibreboard is coloured through the core of the material, so if scratched or dented by flying toys the damage can easily be repaired.

Cork Chair
Hettler Tüllmann
(Katja Hettler & Jula Tüllmann)

Cork, rattan
H: 70 cm (27½ in), W: 88 cm (34⅝ in), D: 90 cm (35⅜ in)

www.hettlertullmann.com

Cork oaks can be harvested for their bark every ten years, and have an expected useful life of up to 100 years. The trees prefer dry and unfertile ground and are instrumental in helping protect hot, dry countries from expanding deserts.

The Cork Chair by German design duo Hettler Tüllmann is made of pressed cork balls woven around a rattan structure, with further cork balls inside to create a beanbag that contours to the shape of any individual, creating a perfectly tailored seat. Combining bright tennis-ball greens and yellows graduating into raw cork, the chair unites contemporary aesthetics with the appeal of this traditional, sustainable material.

Recycled Leather Chair
Hettler Tüllmann
(Katja Hettler & Jula Tüllmann)

Recycled leather, steel
H: 77 cm (30¼ in), W: 60 cm (23⅝ in), D: 78 cm (30¾ in)

www.hettlertullmann.com

The Recycled Leather Chair by Hettler Tüllmann is the result of experimenting with sheets of recycled leather and challenging their boundaries. The pair found that cutting simple slits into the semi-rigid sheets enabled them to achieve greater flexibility without sacrificing any of the robustness or warmth of this natural material.

The process of leather recycling employs leftover leather scraps, collected from furniture and shoe factories, and ground to shreds. They are then mixed with water, natural rubber and acacia wood bark. The leather pulp is compressed into sheets and then mechanically processed for size, colour and texture.

Windworks
Merel Karhof

Wood, wool, natural dye
Various sizes

www.merelkarhof.nl

Windworks is a collection of upholstered furniture pieces, in which the wood, upholstery, dyeing and knitting of the yarn are all executed with a free and inexhaustible energy source – the wind.

The project makes use of two well-preserved historic windmills in northern Holland, each of which produces a different raw material: De Kat (The Cat) grinds colouring materials, while the sawmill Het Jonge Schaap (The Young Sheep) saws planks from trees to old Dutch measurements. A third windmill – the Wind Knitting Factory – then knits the yarns, and with each harvest, the wood structures are upholstered.

By setting up a production triptych between three windmills to create a complete and holistic industry, Windworks demonstrates what can be produced with wind power.

Accumulation
Xerock Kim

Birch, bark, indigo
H: 79.4 cm (31¼ in), W: 80 cm (31½ in), D: 30 cm (11¾ in)

www.kimxerock.com

Accumulation is a birch-wood cabinet covered with flakes of naturally dyed bark. According to its designer, Xerock Kim, 'Accumulation aims at dressing hurt trees cut down for furniture manufacture in their intrinsic, natural clothes'. The bark is coloured with natural indigo, employing traditional dyeing techniques. The cabinet is then covered piece by piece until there is a dense accumulation.

The piece aims to symbolize the point where tradition and modernity meet, while also moving the focus away from the furniture and back to the material itself.

Austerity
Lanzaveccia + Wai

Steel, carbohydrates, proteins, sugar, chocolate
Various sizes

lanzavecchia-wai.com

Austerity is a conceptual furniture project by design duo Lanzaveccia + Wai, exploring the potential role of edible furniture in times of crisis. The designers believe that in situations where once-appreciated decorative elements have become superfluous, these elements could evolve to reflect a new era of austerity – and offer themselves to be consumed when needed.

The furniture consists of metal frames, built to support panels composed of basic nutrients, in the form of carbohydrates, proteins, sugar and chocolate. The panels act as food reserves, while also complementing and completing the objects.

Accordion Table

La Quercia 21
(Luca De Pascalis &
Nicola Gubiotti)

Various woods
Various sizes

www.laquercia21.it

La Quercia 21 is a company born from an encounter between two carpenters – it is a design craft lab and an eclectic box of ideas. Using a combination of various sustainable wood species, scrap materials from old furniture and fixtures, wooden floors and used building construction wood, the duo produce unique pieces of furniture and decorative accessories. Each piece is laboriously crafted by hand, combining joints, mosaics, carvings and lacquers. The products are then treated with natural oil finishes, water and beeswax.

Named for its resemblance to 'a kind of drunken keyboard that compresses and relaxes itself untidily', the top of the Accordion Table is composed of various contrasting woods, cut into irregular widths. It is supported on turned legs made of cherry wood.

Credenza Rossa
La Quercia 21
(Luca De Pascalis & Nicola Gubiotti)

Oak, reclaimed wood, water-based lacquer
Various sizes

www.laquercia21.it

Design duo La Quercia 21 take pleasure in using a diverse combination of woods in their work – including scrap materials salvaged from old furniture, wooden floors and construction sites – and reusing it to create something beautiful and useful (see also page 79).

Their storage pieces are characterized by naive contemporary design, while also recalling the look of 'grandma's kitchen'. The Credenza Rossa is a red lacquered sideboard base with an oak top and front panels made from recycled materials.

Horst
Lasfera

Oiled ash, wool felt
H: 35.5 cm (14 in), W: 30 cm (11¾ in), D: 21 cm (8¼ in)

lasfera.de

Horst is a classic milking stool, given a modern interpretation and a new home. Bringing the stool out of the cowshed and into the home, Lasfera found the pattern for Horst with a small family firm in northern Germany who have been hand-manufacturing similar designs since 1895.

Although the traditional trapezoid shape of the seat has been maintained, it has been brought up to date with a felt covering, available in a range of shades. There is also a version with holes in the felt to expose the traditional wedged joints where the legs join the seat.

Lollygagger Lounge
Loll Designs

Recycled polyethylene (milk containers),
stainless steel fasteners, brass inserts
H: 75 cm (29½ in), W: 68.5 cm (27 in), D: 75 cm (29½ in)

www.lolldesigns.com

The Lollygagger Lounge is made from solid, high-density polyethylene (HDPE), and is 100 per cent recycled and recyclable. HDPE is used to make milk containers and the Lollygagger contains 312 of them, melted down and repurposed. This means it can be left outdoors all year round and is impervious to damp or rot, ensuring a lengthy, maintenance-free life.

If it does get warm outside, there is an integrated bottle opener hidden underneath the right armrest for opening refreshments.

Mill Table
Mater (Thomas Lykke & Ayush Kasliwal)

Recycled teak wood, cast recycled aluminium
H: 74 cm (29⅛ in) L: 200 cm (78¾ in), D: 100 cm (39⅜ in)

mater.dk

The wooden top of the Mill Table is created from materials salvaged from old mill buildings in Jaipur, India, demolished to make space for modern factories.

At first glance, the table displays an essential, modern aesthetic, yet the underside is left raw and unrestored, revealing something of its previous incarnation to anyone who wishes to look a little more closely.

The designers reflect that while they cannot control the destruction of old buildings, they can at least make sure that the remains are put to good use, in a new and sustainable form – a form that celebrates history, and can take these materials into the future.

Brodgar Straw Back Chair
Gareth Neal & Kevin Gauld

Oak, oat straw
H: 81 cm (31⅞ in), W: 61 cm (24 in), D: 56 cm (22 in)

garethneal.co.uk
www.thenewcraftsmen.com

Gareth Neal's Brodgar Straw Back Chair combines a Windsor chair vernacular with the traditional Orkney straw back and pull-out drawer beneath the seat. This contemporary version was constructed from oak and oat straw with the assistance of Kevin Gauld, one of only two remaining traditional Orkney chairmakers.

The Orkney Islands are a treeless archipelago off the north coast of Scotland where wood has always been inevitably scarce. Weaving the back of chairs with straw was therefore a necessary means of making small amounts of scavenged driftwood go a little further, as well as providing a little extra warmth and comfort.

Neal hopes that the simple story of the Brodgar Straw Back Chair is one that could ground designers and craftsmen in their approach to materials, locality and process.

For more on Gareth Neal, see the Q&A on page 86.

Cone
Rentaro Nishimura & Mango Club for People of the Sun

Palm leaves
Outer stool, H: 27 cm (10⅝ in), Diam.: 40 cm (15¾ in)
Inner stool, H: 20 cm (7⅞ in), Diam.: 26 cm (10¼ in)

www.peopleofthesun.net

Replicating the technique and concept of traditional handmade baskets, Cone is a series of stacking stools made by Mango Club from woven palm leaves. The club is a group of artisans in Malawi, brought together by non-profit social enterprise, People of the Sun, whose aim is to help low-income craftworkers gain exposure and create sustainable businesses. This is aided by collaborations with international designers such as Rentaro Nishimura, the London-based designer of the Cone stools. Nishimura brought fresh thinking to the artisans, conceiving new applications for their bespoke, naturally dyed crafts.

Q&A: Gareth Neal

Furniture has always been Gareth Neal's passion, combined with a love for making things. After studying 3D design and craftsmanship, he sold several pieces, which gave him the self-confidence to continue with his passion. He set up a workshop and design studio in 2002 in the East End of London where he creates work in wood ranging from collector's pieces and private commissions to production pieces.

www.garethneal.co.uk

The curved back of the Brodgar Straw Back Chair is designed to protect the user from draughts.

Neal hand weaves the straw using traditional techniques.

How would you describe your style?

My varied practice seeks a reconsideration of furniture design and our perceptions of the contemporary, by questioning history and processes in relation to people and place. The work is positioned at an intersecting point between design and craft, evading any simple categorization into a specific discipline. This approach provides a critical framework for my ideas as the designs develop into new and diverse territory.

In what way is your work sustainable?

As my business now focuses on the medium of wood, and I make very small volumes of furniture, I find it much easier to consider elements of my practice sustainable, though purchasing my timber locally and using only sustainably managed UK-grown timber isn't enough to justify some of my products as sustainable. Within my work I have attempted to produce products that question and challenge the traditional routes to market that the furniture industry uses, trying to remove elements that use high volumes of carbon, returning to green woodland production, using traditional straw-weaving technique and delivery via bicycle in an attempts to make reduce products' carbon footprint.

What materials and techniques do you use?

The techniques I use are varied in relation to the production and design of an object. I try to challenge my decisions continually, to ensure that my designs provoke and question areas around sustainability. This might be through using minimal amount of materials as possible, or the way I might deliver an object, the locality of the manufacturers that I collaborate with, or the people and companies that I collaborate with, or even retail the object through.

What are you working on at the moment, and what do you hope to work on in the future?

I am presently working in collaboration with a farrier to extend his product range and ensure the survival of his craft in a modern world. By working within a pre-established business a designer has the potential to provide growth and look at a business in a way that is impossible for the directors. The outcomes have the potential breath new life, create change.

Have you noticed any particular trends in sustainable design?

Fix it... Repair it... Restore it... Reuse it... But this should not be a trend!

What materials or techniques do you think we'll be seeing more of in the future?

Obviously rapid prototyping is becoming more and more accessible, but serious consideration is needed in regards to whether every home should have a 3D printer in their house – is this really beneficial for the environment? How many devices have you thrown away?

As part of Neal's In Pursuit of Carbon Negative challenge, he cycled to a woodland in Herefordshire and made furniture in situ from felled trees. He slept outdoors and ate locally, with the aim of producing furniture without carbon emissions.

Reeds
Odd Matter (Els Woldhek & Georgi Manassiev)

Reeds, oak
Various sizes

oddmatterstudio.com

Odd Matter made their first reed table for a client in the Netherlands, who lived in a small village of traditional thatched-roofs farmhouses, surrounded by wetlands. The reeds were grown on the surrounding land and bought from the local thatcher, only a few hundred metres from the client's house. The oak used for the tabletop came from the local boat builder, who builds traditional all-wooden boats to help the locals get around the village.

The designers were keen to work with materials found in the immediate environment, and to realize the potential of reeds, used throughout the world in an endless variety of ways.

Shanes Lounger
Oxgut Hose Co.

Recycled fire hose, steel
H: 86.4 cm (34 in), W: 78.7 cm (31 in), D: 179 cm (70½ in)

oxgut.com
childburn.org

Comprising a continuous length of recycled hose wrapped around a steel frame, Shanes Lounger is named after two US fire captains of the same name.

US fire departments discard their hoses once they are no longer in perfect condition, and California-based manufacturers Oxgut rescue literally tonnes of these hoses from landfill each year. Making use of their bold colours, worn character and still-considerable strength, they are then transformed into a range of products (see also page 247). In addition, a portion of Oxgut's annual proceeds are donated to the Children's Burn Foundation.

R Toddler Bed
and F Bunk Bed
RaFa-kids (Agata
& Arek Seredyn)

FSC-certified birch plywood
Toddler bed, L: 205 cm (80¾ in), W: 95 cm (37⅜ in)
Bunk bed, L: 155 cm (61 in), W: 75 cm (29½ in)

www.rafa-kids.com

RaFa-kids think of a child's bed as not just a place to sleep, but as a playful and functional element in a room. Both of these beds are designed to encourage play, creativity and beauty while remaining functional and safe.

Constructed from sustainably sourced European birch plywood and machined using the latest CNC technology, each part is produced with maximum efficiency, in an effort to reduce waste to virtually zero. The beds are finished with two layers of water-based Scandinavian lacquers and flat-packed for efficient transportation. They are non-toxic, low-VOC and 100 per cent free of HAPs (hazardous air pollutants).

Rope Stool
Yoav Reches

Recycled plastic eco sheet, hemp rope
Various sizes

yoav-reches.com

The Rope Stool was developed as designer Yoav Reches's graduation project at the Royal College of Art, London. It consists of flat panels of 100 per cent recycled HDPE plastic sheet, held together by braided hemp rope to create tension. The sheet material is manufactured from mixed low-grade waste plastics, which are notoriously hard to recycle and are normally incinerated or consigned to landfill. The rope is guided through a pattern of grooves snaking across the different faces, binding the elements in a rigid embrace.

The Rope Stool provides an alternative to flat-pack furniture, offering a simple, tool-free assembly process, while also avoiding the need for fixings or adhesives.

Weatherboard Trestle Table
Rekindle

Scrapwood
H: 74 cm (29⅛ in), L: 80 cm (31½ in), W: 76 cm (29⅞ in)

www.rekindle.org.nz

The Weatherboard Trestle Table is made from ancient slow-growing indigenous New Zealand timber, mainly rimu, felled at an unsustainable level in the early 1900s to build homes. Rekindle work on the principle that since these forests are now protected, this kind of timber will never be available again; it is therefore important to harness what is left of this culturally significant material (see also page 302).

The table is made with weatherboards and framing, salvaged by local community organizations from over 7,000 homes being demolished in earthquake-stricken Christchurch. Rekindle are fighting to save as much of this timber as possible, using it as the basis for all their products before it is consigned to landfill.

Chest of Drawers
Tejo Remy for Droog

Used drawers, maple, jute strap
H: 120cm (47¼ in), L: 110cm (43¼ in), W: 60cm (23⅝ in) (variable)

www.droog.com

Chest of Drawers had its premiere in 1991 and has since become a true icon of sustainable design. Collected by museums such as the Museum of Modern Art and the Museum of Arts and Design in New York, the piece explores reuse and reappropriation, and is a criticism of overproduction and consumerism.

Designer Tejo Remy collected found drawers, gave them new enclosures and loosely bundled them together into a chest. The chest has no fixed form, and the drawers can be combined and exchanged at will, encouraging us to make our own paradise with what we encounter.

Turned Tables
Magnus Scholz
for WorkHouse

Oak
Small, H: 46 cm (18⅛ in), D: 34 cm (13⅜ in)
Medium, H: 58 cm (22⅞ in), D: 34 cm (13⅜ in)
Large, H: 70 cm (27⅝ in), D: 34 cm (13⅜ in)

workhousecollection.co.uk

Designed by Magnus Scholz for WorkHouse and inspired by eighteenth-century garden urns, this family of crude yet elegant side tables are made in the UK from a single log of 'green' English oak. Shaped by hand on an old-fashioned lathe, they are then left to dry out naturally, allowing cracks and splits to appear, making each one unique.

Lou P.
Stephen Shaheen

Marble
H: 91 cm (36 in), W: 76 cm (30 in), D: 71 cm (28 in)

stephenshaheen.com

Lou P. is a sculptural chair made from 22 layers of Botticino marble, made with discarded remnants left over from industrial stone fabrication. Each thin segment is delicately cut from marble remainders, laminated together and hand-finished to create the chair's smooth and sinuous form. Lou P. exhibits a particularly extreme level of upcycling, producing a genuine luxury item from waste materials that will be around for many years to come.

Metrobench
Stephen Shaheen

NYC MetroCards, steel
L: 107 cm (42 in), W: 46 cm (18 in), D: 46 cm (18 in)

stephenshaheen.com

Metrobench is a sculptural bench, made from hundreds of recycled New York City MetroCards laminated on to a sheet steel. Shaheen was inspired to use these discarded objects to represent thousands of different journeys converging into a single moment, reflecting the manner in which mass transit joins many diverse lives.

The bench was assembled completely by hand, card by card. Using Craigslist, Stephen harnessed the people of New York to help him gather 5,000 MetroCards in under a week. 'There is something very personal about handling so many small belongings that were once riding around in people's pockets. There are untold personal stories in that inconspicuous, flimsy plastic.'

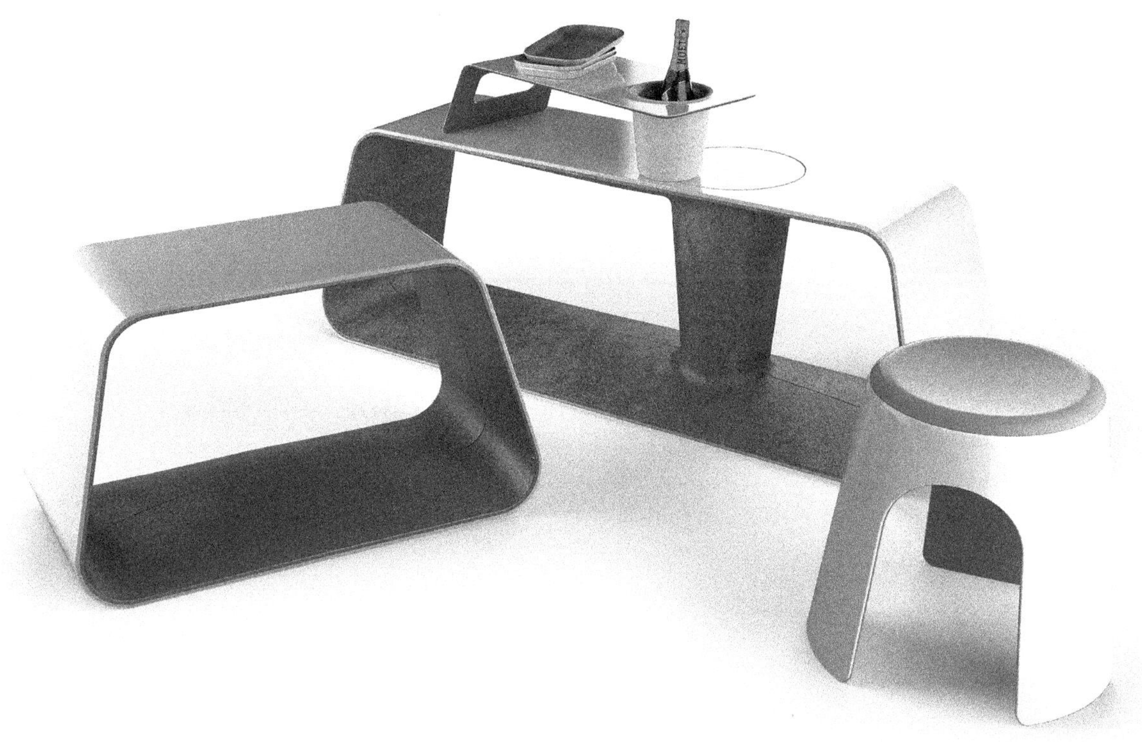

Re:composed
Springtime with Pols Potten and NPSP

Car waste, clothing, agricultural waste
Various sizes

www.springtime.nl
www.polspotten.nl
www.npsp.nl

The Re:composed project focuses on using unrecycled scrapped cars, shredded clothing fabric and agricultural waste as a base for luxurious, premium interior products. These materials are broken down and then reconstituted into a laminated composite. The outer layer has a slick white finish while the interior displays the fibres, speckles, grain and desaturated tones of its individual recycled ingredients.

The dual surfaces demonstrate not only what is capable of being recycled, but also just how fresh and sleek those materials can become, worthy of being used in even the most high-end products.

Broom Chair
Philippe Starck for Emeco

Reclaimed WPP, reclaimed wood fibre
H: 83 cm (32⅝ in), W: 48 cm (18⅞ in), D: 50 cm (19⅝ in)

www.emeco.net

Emeco has a history of making beautiful furniture from recycled materials. The company continues to search for new ways to recover discarded materials and use them to make products that last, improving the earth for future generations.

Emeco and Philippe Starck came together to create a chair that is reclaimed, repurposed, recyclable – and designed to last. The Broom stacking chair is made from 75 per cent waste polypropylene and 15 per cent reclaimed wood fibre, which would normally be swept into the trash. 'Imagine,' says Starck, 'a guy who takes a humble broom and starts to clean the workshop and with this dust he makes new magic. That's why we call it the Broom Chair.'

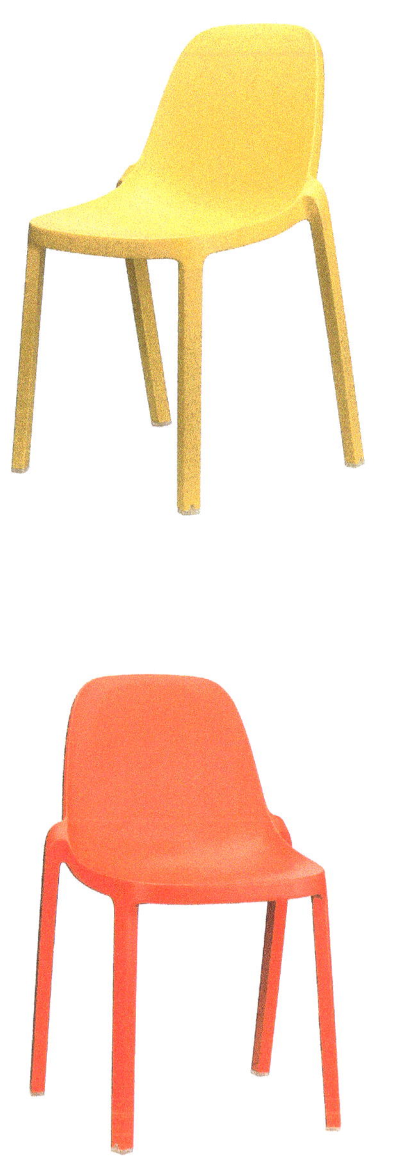

Chair Farm
Studio Aisslinger

Bamboo, steel, glass
Various sizes

www.aisslinger.de

The Chair Farm prototype envisages furniture that is grown rather than produced, and harvested locally rather than exported globally. The concept is as simple as it is radical. The chair is no longer produced in the classical sense of the word. Instead, it grows of its own volition in a greenhouse or a field – a production utopia of the future.

Plants are trained inside a metal mould; when they reach maturity, the steel corset is opened and removed, revealing a naturally grown chair. Designer Werner Aisslinger describes this as 'a new way to invert production in furniture design back from globalized serial manufacturing to resource-conserving local production.'

Hemp Chair
Studio Aisslinger with BASF

Hemp, kenaf
H: 74 cm (29⅛ in), W: 74 cm (29⅛ in), D: 66 cm (26 in)

www.aisslinger.de

At the 2011 Ventura Lambrate exhibition 'Poetry Happens', Werner Aisslinger presented the world's first concept for a monobloc chair made of natural fibres – a project supported by the German chemical company BASF. The Hemp Chair was designed for a lightweight manufacturing process stemming from the car industry: the renewable raw materials (hemp and kenaf) are compressed with a water-based thermoset binder to form an eco-friendly, lightweight and yet strong composite.

The chair is designed in the tradition of monobloc stackable chairs, which have often been made of reinforced plastics. The sustainable sheet material of the Hemp Chair, however, allows the use of more than 70 per cent natural fibres in combination with BASF's water-based acrylic resin, Acrodur. Unlike with classic reactive resins, no chemicals are released during the cross-linking process; the only by-product of the curing procedure is water. Furthermore, the industrial process of compression moulding allows the low-cost mass production of three-dimensional objects with high mechanical resistance and very low specific weight.

Bust Chair
Studiŏ Libertíny (Tomás Gabzdil Libertíny) with the Henraux Foundation

Marble
H: 75 cm (29½ in), W: 63 cm (24¾ in), D: 71 cm (28 in)

www.studiolibertiny.com

The Henraux Foundation is a company with a cutting-edge approach to marble production and a long history of cooperation with leading global artists such as Henry Moore, Hans Arp and Isamu Noguchi. Their facility seeks to produce marble as sustainably as possible, contributes waste material to road building, and collects and supplies marble dust for industrial use.

Produced in collaboration with sculptors at the Henraux Foundation, the Bust Chair by Tomás Gabzdil Libertíny is hewn from a solid block of white Carrara marble. Destined to last for centuries, the Bust Chair is not going to be in landfill any time soon.

Help Me Darwin
Studio NOCC
(Juan Pablo Naranjo)

Cardboard
Various sizes

www.nocc.fr
www.19greekstreet.com

Help Me Darwin is a versatile corrugated-cardboard furniture kit designed for habitat emergencies. From a bag containing locally sourced cardboard, you can build a folding screen, which can then be transformed into a bed, a table and three stools. The kit is designed to adapt easily to empty spaces, and the carry bag itself unfolds to become the bed's mattress.

The piece demonstrates how ten simple sheets of cardboard can functionally mimic furniture as we know it.

LeafBed
Studio NOCC
(Juan Pablo Naranjo)
with Leaf Supply

Cardboard
Various sizes

www.nocc.fr
www.leafsupply.com

The LeafBed is a patented camp bed made entirely from cardboard – a simple, efficient and ecological temporary housing solution. Leaf Supply produces locally in order to be able to supply with reactivity and flexibility. The LeafBed is an adaptable design, assembled from four identical modules with alternative uses: four modules create an adult bed, three modules create a child's bed, two modules create a small table, and one module creates a stool.

The bed's strength relies on the perfect mix of an inner structure with an outer envelope, which creates 'building blocks', allowing the bed to resist loads of up to 900 kg (1980 lb) with the use of as little as 7 kg (15 lb) of cardboard.

The LeafBed is a simple and economical way of creating a sense of home in less 'settled' situations. It is also easy to transport and recycle.

Tofu
Leonardo Talarico

Tofu

leonardotalarico.com

Tofu is a descriptively named armchair by Italian designer Leonardo Talarico. Dried slices of this unusual construction material are grafted together like shingles into an austere, geometric form.

Tofu is a soft, nutrient-rich and ancient foodstuff. However, following a dehydration process and subsequent thermal shock, it gains important mechanical properties and can readily be used as a structural material. The armchair is then treated with a natural coating that is able to change colour depending on the reactive acidity of the material.

Bloomberg Chair
Nina Tolstrup for
19 Greek Street

Scrap pine wood
H: 132 cm (52 in), W: 49.5 cm (19½ in), D: 54 cm (21¼ in)

www.19greekstreet.com

The 'Waste Not, Want It' exhibition is an annual event hosted by news agency Bloomberg, displaying the latest in a series of specially commissioned art and design projects created for Bloomberg Philanthropy by consultancy Arts Co. It commissions artists and designers to create furniture, lighting and installations almost entirely out of the waste from Bloomberg's own London office in order to question why useful but redundant wood is often regarded as waste.

Tolstrup dismantled and kiln-dried 250 used pallets, transforming them into a round conference table and chairs using high-end cabinet-making techniques.

Box Day Bed
Mark Tuckey

FSC-certified oak or FSC-certified Douglas fir, fabric
L: 240 cm (94½ in), W: 100 cm (39⅜ in), H: 75 cm (29½ in)

www.marktuckey.com.au

The Box Day Bed is a minimal but comfortable sofa, crafted in sustainable timber by Mark Tuckey. The sofa is available in either FSC-certified Douglas fir or oak, and can be upholstered in any fabric.

Tuckey has been making sustainable furniture in Australia for 25 years, having started out by recycling timber picked up from building sites. His company now employs 45 people, but he still believes strongly in using only sustainable plantations or recycled timber to minimize the company's eco footprint in the future. This commitment also extends to remaking and repairing furniture for existing customers, to ensure a long life of contented use.

Birds
Lucy Turner

Teak, Formica
Various sizes

www.lucyturner.co

Lucy Turner specializes in transforming mid-century furniture with sheets of Formica laminate, laser-cut with her own designs, such as pineapples, birds or flamingo motifs.

Each piece is painstakingly inlayed using Formica laminate manufactured in the UK. A highly practical material, it is resistant to impact, heat and scratches, and requires minimal maintenance, providing a long-lasting finish.

Turner often finds herself saving furniture from disposal by customizing and updating pieces that could be seen as rather dated, creating a finished result is 'a perfect balance of contemporary and retro'.

Malawi Chair
Tyanjane Club for People of the Sun

Local wood, bamboo and water reeds, bicycle wheel
H: 85 cm (33½ in), W: 80 cm (31½ in), L: 55 cm (21⅝ in)

www.peopleofthesun.net

The Tyanjane Club is a group of artisans in Malawi, supported by the non-profit social enterprise People of the Sun. The Tyanjane Club use locally sourced bamboo and water reeds to construct an updated range of traditional Malawian chairs in a vibrant, contemporary colour palette. The sweeping curve of the seat is formed from the rims of worn-out bicycle wheels.

People of the Sun unite global designers with native craftworkers in Africa to exchange inspiration and information between their different creative processes, maximizing the appeal of traditional craft skills in a modern, international context (see also pages 85, 250).

Well Proven Chair
Marjan van Aubel
& Jamie Shaw

Foaming wood
H: 75 cm (29½ in), W: 45 cm (17¾ in), D: 45 cm (17¾ in)

www.marjanvanaubel.com

Calculating that there is 50 to 80 per cent timber wastage during normal furniture manufacture, Marjan van Aubel and Jamie Shaw (supported by the American Hardwood Export Council and Benchmark Furniture) began to explore ways of incorporating waste shavings into a chair design.

Discovering a foaming chemical reaction on mixing the shavings with bio-resin, the designers were able to add dye and create a colourful, lightweight and mouldable material, reinforced by the variously sized shreds of wood fibre. The porridge-like mixture of resin and shavings was then applied to the underside of a chair shell by hand, building up the material wherever extra strength was required. The mixture then foamed explosively to create its own exuberant form, anchored by simple turned legs of American ash.

The chairs produced during this project will be some of the first pieces of furniture subjected to life cycle analysis (LCA), an important tool for measuring and comparing environmental impacts of manufactured goods.

For more on Marjan van Aubel, see the Q&A on page 110.

Furniture

Q&A: Marjan van Aubel

Marjan van Aubel never set out to be a product designer, but became increasingly interested in it during her studies in the designLAB programme at the Gerrit Rietveld Academie in Amsterdam. She went on to graduate in Design Products at the Royal College of Art in London. She now works on furniture projects that incorporate sustainable energy.

www.marjanvanaubel.com

Van Aubel's Energy Collection uses natural dyes to create currents of electricity.

How would you describe your style?

It is very much research based and that is also the part I enjoy the most, I really do like to collaborate with other parties. This can be other designers, companies or institutions in completely different fields from design. On those collaborations I do have my own – very inquisitive – style and I stamp in it. I study materials and their behaviour, and I try to manipulate them in different ways in order to create something new and then work from the material itself. As a researcher, I am curious about what appear to be ordinary things and processes, and I am always looking for new links between them.

In what way is your work sustainable?

In my work I really consider the material, the way it has been made and its use. I try to work from the material itself. Sustainability is a thing that must be part of the design and as considered as its function, shape and colour.

What materials and techniques do you use?

I am working with different techniques and materials, and none of them are very conventional. For example I have been developing a foaming porcelain that rises, just like bread, in the kiln and expands itself to about 300% of its original volume. This means you only need one-third of the original material. It has unusual properties: it is extremely lightweight, floats in water and is semi-translucent. The production of foam porcelain is completely different from that of normal porcelain and goes against all ceramic rules. There is an experimental boundary between controlling the material while also letting it behave freely, which I very much enjoy.

Same with the Well Proven series of chairs (see page 109), which are made from a combination of bioresin and sawdust that also starts a foaming reaction and expands. We came up with a way to get the seat literally growing onto the legs using a jig.

For the Energy Collection (see page 264) I collaborated with a company called Solaronix that is working on a dye sensitized solar cell, which uses colour to generate an electrical current. The cells look like coloured stain glass and I implement their technologies into usable objects.

What are you working on at the moment, and what do you hope to work on in the future?

At the moment I am working on a solar-cell table with Solaronix that will have one big solar cell as its top surface. That means the whole tabletop, as well as being a usable table, will charge during the day and store energy that can then be used to charge your phone or any other electrical device. I really like the idea that objects are self-sufficient and get an extra double function.

Have you noticed any particular trends in sustainable design?

There is a lot of material research going on now. Lots of research into new bioplastics – chairs made from mushrooms or milk, for example. I hope some of these experiments will reach a bigger market and really have an impact.

What materials or techniques do you think we'll be seeing more of in the future?

I hope we will see more techniques like the dye synthesized solar cells. I think it's very important that innovative technologies are designed in such away that they are attractive and nice to look at. At the moment, I think solar cells are being used in a very poor way, just stacked onto roofs. It would be nice, for example, if there were solar-cell roof tiles that could be clicked into the roof. New technologies, like the dye synthesized solar cells, should be combined with design and aesthetics.

Q&A: Marjan van Aubel

The Well Proven Series is made from a mixture of resin and waste wood shavings. The material foams to create its own exuberant form.

Color Collision
Kirstie van Noort
& Rogier Arents

Porcelain, ash wood, cabbage dye
H: 40 cm (15¾ in), Diam.: 50 cm (19⅝ in)

www.kirstievannoort.nl
rogierarents.nl

Color Collision is a collection of non-toxic ceramics designed by Kirstie van Noort and Rogier Arents, which includes this porcelain-topped side table. To achieve the unique colours, the pieces were first dyed with red cabbage extracts and then soaked in various liquids with different pH levels.

Uniting Van Noort's research into materials and processes with Arents' scientific approach, the project hopes to reveal how non-toxic pigments can be used in everyday designs, and how simple, natural reactions can lead to striking, original results.

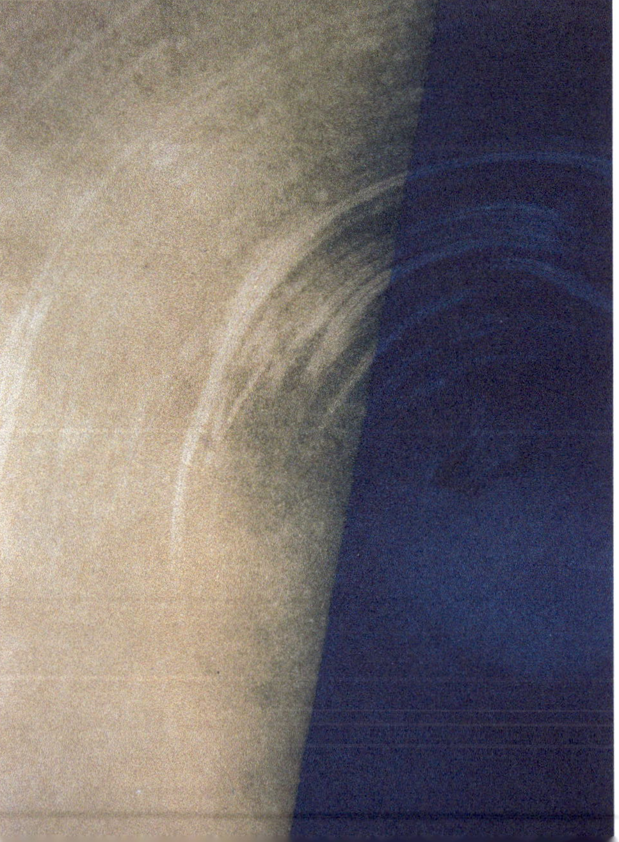

Nomad
VE2 with Skagerak

FSC-certified oak
H: 194 cm (76⅜ in), W: 55 cm (21⅝ in), D: 3.5 cm (1⅜ in)

www.skagerak.dk

In collaboration with the design trio VE2, Danish furniture manufacturer Skagerak has developed Nomad, a verstile and unusual storage unit, crafted from FSC-certified oak.

Nomad is easy to move and can be used in various capacities, in any room, or even outside. It can also be customized with supplementary shelves and hooks to fulfil new functions.

Skagerak aspire to consider the needs of coming generations by creating long-lasting furniture which can be repaired simply and will not need replacing for many years. This approach ensures a reduced demand on materials, energy and transport. The company aim to source timber from as close as possible to their factory and account for ease of flat-packing in their design process, further reducing shipping requirements and their associated effects.

Dean Credenza
Volk (Brian Volk-Zimmerman)

Ash, brass, linen, natural oils, wax
Dresser, H: 76.2 cm (30 in), W: 152.4 cm (60 in), D: 5 cm (2 in)
Hutch, H: 106.7 cm (42 in), W: 132 cm (52 in), D: 31.8 cm (12½ in)

www.volkfurniture.com

Handmade in Brooklyn, New York, the Dean Credenza is a distinctive, minimalist dresser crafted from FSC-certified ash, finished with low-VOC oils. The sliding panel doors are upholstered in linen, and decorated with brightly coloured, hand-painted trapezoids and triangles, embellishing the herringbone fabric.

Employing small recycled touches, maker Brian Volk-Zimmerman repurposes discarded men's shirting fabric, salvaged from local clothing manufacturers, to line the inside of each drawer. Previous designs have also made use of typewriter keys and pump organ draw knobs.

Volk-Zimmerman believes that the primary consideration for sustainability in furniture is ensuring that each piece is made to last – not just decades, but generations. Emphasizing this notion, the company is named in honour of his great-great-great-great grandfather, John Volk, a furniture maker of local renown in the early nineteenth century, whose furniture is still used by his descendants.

Windsor Rocker
Katie Walker

Ash
H: 81 cm (31⅞ in), W: 72 cm (28⅜ in), D: 102 cm (40⅛ in)

www.katiewalkerfurniture.com

The Windsor Rocker is Katie Walker's unique update
of perhaps the most quintessential of all English furniture
designs. Light, strong and elegant, the Windsor chair
has been popular since the 1720s, when it was originally
painted green and used as a garden seat prior to
moving indoors in its more familiar guise as an unpainted,
polished-wood household staple. Over the years the
design has evolved from a simple country chair to
a more sophisticated piece.

Made from locally grown sustainable ash and treated
with a natural oil-based finish, the wood is worked green,
meaning it has not been kiln-dried prior to its production.
Apart from furniture-making skills, the rocker is also a
further development of the wheelwright's craft expressed
in a chair. The continuous band of ash forming the frame
pushes the possibilities of steam bending to its limit.

T-Shirt Chair
Maria Westerberg for
Green Furniture Sweden

Powder-coated steel, cotton
H: 77.8 cm (30⅝ in), W: 50 cm (19⅝ in), D: 100 cm (39⅜ in)

greenfurniture.se

Resembling a traditional Swedish rag rug, the T-Shirt Chair is a contoured, steel-wired frame, into which the owner can weave their own worn-out clothes and fabrics to create a unique, personalized piece of furniture.

Over time textiles can be individually replaced, allowing the chair to evolve, be repaired and present an ongoing history of the owner's wardrobe. In fact, as long as it is used indoors, the frame has a lifetime guarantee.

The chair can also be supplied ready-upholstered with recycled scraps from the same factory in a selected all-colour mix.

Paperpulp Cabinets
Debbie Wijskamp

Recycled newspaper, water-based binder
Various sizes

www.debbiewijskamp.com

Debbie Wijskamp's Paperpulp Cabinets are created from simple building blocks of interlocking papier mâché, assembled into drawers and shelves with water-based glue.

Drawing her inspiration from traditional cultures who make their homes with locally sourced materials, the Dutch designer began to experiment with discarded newspapers, found in abundance in modern Arnhem. Mashing the paper into pulp and leaving it to dry into moulded components, Wijskamp was able to create furniture that does indeed recall native architecture, from igloos to Inca cities.

Ay Illuminate · Baan · Henry Baumann · Tord Boontje · Valentina Carretta · Alvaro Catalán de Ocón · Sebastian Cox · Tania da Cruz · David Trubridge · DesignByThem · Designtree · Ekobo · Ett La Benn · Facaro · Lars Beller Fjetland · Emiliano Godoy · David Graas · Herrwolke · Hettler Tüllmann · Pepe Heykoop · Benjamin Hubert · IKEA · La Quercia 21 · Lasfera · Tamara Maynes · Sergio Mendoza · MFEO · Herminia Mira · Molo · Nir Meiri Design Studio · Nonage · Original House · Naomi Paul · Jake Phipps · Pia Design · Karim Rashid · Rawstudio · The Red Dog · Roman & Williams · Peter Schumacher · Secto Design · Stephen Shaheen · Nikolaj Steenfatt · Strand Design · Studio Schneemann · Supercyclers & Blakebrough + King · Sep Verboom · Henry Wilson

Lighting

Umut Lights
Ay Illuminate

Rattan
H: 121 cm (47⅝ in), Diam.: 30 or 35 cm (11¾ or 13¾ in)

www.ayilluminate.com

Ay Illuminate are a Dutch lighting company who work with artisans in Asia and Africa to create 'contemporary, organically shaped designs, created by local techniques in natural materials'. Their Umat lampshades are made in Southeast Asia from rattan, and use a minimal amount of material to create a large and light structure similar to a fishing trap.

By working with local craftworkers, the company are able to understand the traditional local materials and handcraft expertise specific to each area. This helps them to find the best method of combining these techniques and materials with contemporary design ideas.

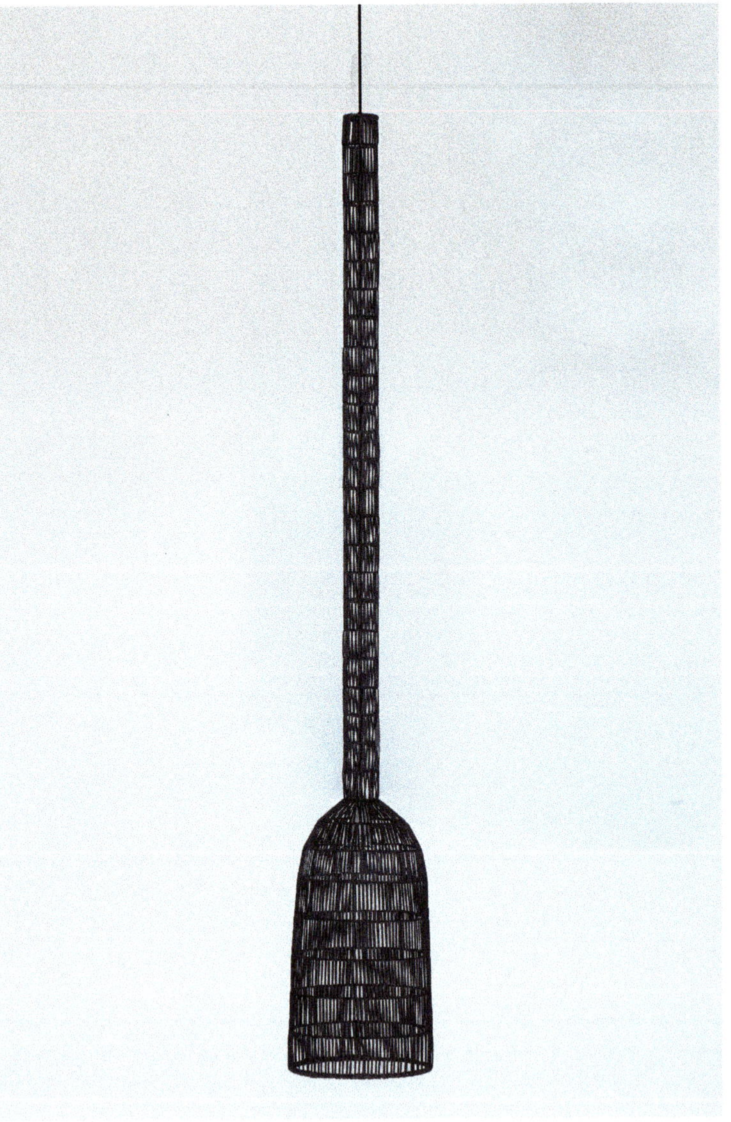

"

Suspension Lights
Baan

Bamboo
Various sizes

www.baan-baan.com

Parisian company Baan, which means 'home' in Thai, aims to design 'unpretentious everyday objects', notable for their usefulness, history and raw materials.

Handcrafted from sustainable bamboo, Baan's suspension lights are simple, basket-like shapes employing a variety of weaving techniques to create different styles of open mesh.

The company believe in small-scale production, and in noble and natural materials, to promote traditional handcrafts and create an atmosphere of 'simplicity, peacefulness and nature'.

130
Henry Baumann

Wooden fruit boxes
Various sizes

www.henrybaumann.de

This project consists of a lamp and accompanying furniture made from 130 wooden boxes collected at the Maastricht fruit market in the Netherlands. Normally these would be thrown away everyday, but by removing the staples, Baumann has found they can be disassembled to create the building blocks of new items.

Although 130 has saved material from landfill, the designer is more interested in demonstrating the possibilities of this modular system, where waste can be broken down and put back together again in a new form, using the same staples it was held together with in the first place.

Come Rain Come Shine
Tord Boontje for Artecnica

Metal, cotton, organza, silk
Small, H: 95 cm (37⅜ in), Diam.: 40 cm (15¾ in)
Medium, H: 135 cm (53⅛ in), Diam.: 60 cm (23⅝ in)
Large, H: 165 cm (65 in), Diam.: 76 cm (29⅞ in)

www.artecnicainc.com

Come Rain Come Shine is Tord Boontje's reinterpretation of the chandelier, produced through Coopa-Roca, a women's cooperative based in Rio de Janeiro's largest shanty town. By using their homes as workshops, cooperative members earn a living while tending to their children and other domestic responsibilities.

Artecnica's Design With Conscience campaign is a programme to promote self-sustaining communities of talented artisans in underdeveloped areas. It is founded on the premise that the value of artisan-made goods has always been appreciated, but with the globalization of trade, artisans have become divorced from their traditional markets, isolating them from the potential demand for their craft.

By introducing designers and project producers into communities, Artecnica are able to bring the work of the designer and the artisan to the consumer. They aim to avoid assembly-line production, exploitation of third-world labour, and the displacement of workers that often results from large organizations with global reach.

Egg of Columbus
Valentina Carretta
with Fabrica for Seletti

Paper pulp
Diam.: 22.5 cm (8⅞ in)

www.valentinacarretta.it
www.seletti.it

Designer Valentina Carretta's Egg of Columbus is a lampshade constructed from coarse, moisture-resistant reycled paper. Aiming to combine contemporary design with eco-friendly practices, the lamp makes use of the type of coarse paper material used for egg cartons, giving it a distinctive yet humble appearance.

The lampshade's name refers to the story of how explorer Christopher Columbus challenged his detractors to make an egg stand on its tip. When they gave up, he did it himself by tapping the egg on a table to flatten its tip, demonstrating how a brilliant idea can seem easy once you know how it is done.

PET Lamp
Alvaro Catalán de Ocón

PET plastic
Various sizes

www.petlamp.org
catalandeocon.com

The PET Lamp is the result of a project to find ways of recycling the PET plastic bottles invading every corner of the planet, and to reduce the amount of this waste material polluting our oceans.

To manufacture the design, Alvaro Catalán de Ocón decided to fuse these ubiquitous mass-produced industrial objects with a highly traditional handcraft technique, employing a workshop of artisans in Colombia who had been displaced by guerrilla warfare.

The lampshade is constructed from woven strips of cut plastic, and the neck of the bottle is used to connect with the light fitting, creating an object that gives this durable material a much longer lifespan and keeps it out of the seas.

Rod Desk Light
Sebastian Cox

Coppiced hazel
H: 54 cm (21¼ in), D: 20cm (7⅞ in), W: 12 cm (4¾ in)

sebastiancox.co.uk

Sebastian Cox's Rod Desk Light is testament to the English woodworker's strong belief that 'sustainable design does not have to result in a boring or compromised product'. Combining local materials and traditional techniques with a contemporary aesthetic, the piece employs a steam-bent rod of coppiced hazel for the stem, while the shaggy shade is made from ultra-thin translucent hazel shavings.

For more on Sebastian Cox, see the Q&A on page 128.

Popcork
Tania da Cruz with Amorim

Cork, LEDs

www.taniadacruz.com

Rising demand for natural cork is resulting in soaring prices and sinking quality as pressure builds on limited supplies of this highly appealing material. A related material, expanded cork, makes use of leftover scraps of natural cork that would otherwise be discarded. Expanded cork was developed in the 1990s as a natural and recyclable insulation material that is also waterproof and fireproof. It is also particularly suited to soundproofing, as the expanded cells contain 50 per cent air.

The Popcork lamp by Tania da Cruz is named in tribute to expanded cork, which is produced by heating small pieces of cork until they expand like popcorn, before being fused together with steam.

Q&A: Sebastian Cox

From childhood, Sebastian Cox always had an interest in nature and plants, and his dream jobs were always outside and hands on. His parents' business, Cox Restorations, was a huge influence on him, and he spent a lot time on building sites, fascinated by jowell posts and scarf joints. Sebastian now designs and makes simple, elegant furniture from local British wood, using a combination of traditional craft techniques and contemporary processes.

www.sebastiancox.co.uk

Cox's Pole Bench is made from coppiced hazel, harvested by hand in Lincolnshire, and scorched ash.

How would you describe your style?
My style is honest, and combines traditional techniques
with a contemporary ethos and aesthetic. I keep the
form as simple as possible and allow the timber and
construction to provide the visual detail and interest. I
suppose, to an extent, the furniture is almost a platform
to show off the material and the process.

In what way is your work sustainable?
I only work with British hardwoods, such as oak, sycamore
and ash. I want to do everything possible to encourage
British consumers to specify English hardwoods over
imported. I also work with a lesser-known English
hardwood, called coppiced hazel. Hazel is abundant in
the UK, and coppicing is a process that can provide an
inexhaustible supply of timber without ever replanting.
Essentially, it involves cutting an area of trees at
ground level. Contrary to what you might think about
cutting down a tree, this doesn't kill the hazel tree, but
encourages it to act as a pruned fruit tree does – it bursts
in to life the following spring, throwing up vigorous and
fast-growing shoots from its stumps and root system.

I was determined to find a use for this totally abundant,
renewable, sustainable material. I ended up with a
collection of pieces that use British hardwoods and
hazel sourced as locally to the workshop as possible
(see pages 52, 126, 197). It's important that each piece
underlines my ethos of sustainability.

What materials and techniques do you use?
I work with British hardwoods; predominantly oak,
sycamore, ash and coppiced hazel, sourced from
a wood in Kent, less than 40 miles from my
South East London workshop.

Other timber that I use for bespoke pieces comes from
a fantastic timber mill in Sussex, who specialize in English
hardwoods. It's very hard to find somewhere that can
offer information about what you're buying, including
the provenance of the timber. With my current supplier,
I know most of my timber comes from densely wooded
Sussex and the surrounding South Eastern counties.

**What are you working on at the moment, and what
do you hope to work on in the future?**
I've started to undertake more and more bespoke
commissions in coppiced hazel. I hope this continues
to grow, because it encourages me to venture into
uncharted territory, broadening the potential of
coppiced wood.

I've started to measure the CO_2 released in making my
pieces, which has produced some interesting results, and
I'd like to work on this more, and get the data more and
more accurate. I think being able to give a carbon value
of an item is a really important step towards a sustainable
future, and I'd like to eventually offer it with all of my
pieces.

In the short term I've got some exciting collaborations
with a top retailer, and I hope to explore other coppiced
woods – I've got my eye on chestnut next!

**Have you noticed any particular trends
in sustainable design?**
I hope that there aren't too many trends in sustainable
design. Trends tend to come and go, and I hope
sustainability remains a priority for designers for the
rest of time. In fact, I like the idea that sustainability isn't
enough – I think we could do more than sustain, and
eventually we should aim to improve.

**What materials or techniques do you think
we'll be seeing more of in the future?**
I think natural materials will continue to appeal to
consumers, and I hope designers continue to look to
wood, wool, ceramics, paper, etc. for new ideas.

Manuka
David Trubridge
(Amy Lynch &
David Trubridge)

Bamboo plywood, polycarbonate
Diam.: 80 or 110 cm (31½ or 43¼ in)

www.davidtrubridge.com

Much of designer David Trubridge's work is inspired by his time tramping in the New Zealand bush. Having a connection with nature is central to his ambition to bring cultural nourishment into people's lives without using up precious resources and energy.

The low-energy LED Manuka light began life as a 2D screen based on leaf shapes, until one of his designers, Amy Lynch, took the idea further. By rearranging the shapes, she created the delicate, five-pointed shapes reminiscent of the tiny white flower blossoms of the indigenous manuka tree.

The Manuka uses a small quantity of sustainably sourced bamboo plywood and polycarbonate to create a surprisingly large light, although Trubridge is currently testing and exploring plant-based plastics to replace the oil-based polycarbonate components.

All waste from the factory is sorted and sent to separate recycling facilities, while sawdust is incinerated at a local plant to generate electricity. The Manuka is also designed for easy flat-pack shipping.

WebLight
DesignByThem
(Nicholas Karlovasitis &
Sarah Gibson)

HDPE plastic
Diam.: 55 cm (21⅝ in)

www.designbythem.com

Made from 100 per cent Australian-sourced material, DesignByThem's WebLight takes its name from its silky, natural-looking form, spun from nothing but recycled plastic bags and factory waste. The forming process uses reusable moulds and renewable energy sources to create a finished product which is itself recyclable.

The lamp is built to take a low-energy 30-watt compact fluorescent bulb and is shipped in non-printed cardboard packing. DesignByThem also offer a product stewardship programme, allowing their creations to be returned for repair, reuse or recycling.

Q&A: David Trubridge

David Trubridge loved making things as a child. He studied for a degree in Naval Architecture (Boat Design) and later taught himself the craft of woodworking. Only after mastering that did he start to think about design. Now, with his company David Trubridge Ltd, he designs and manufactures furniture, lighting, jewellery and fabric inspired by his travels and with a strong focus on sustainability.

www.davidtrubridge.com

The Nikau light is named after the only indigenous palm tree in New Zealand. It has a large bulb at the top of its trunk and its leaves, traditionally used for thatching and weaving, overlap in similar patterns.

How would you describe your style?
It is firmly contemporary, but I avoid fashion and styling, if I can. I try to make my designs as classical and timeless as possible so that people won't throw them out too soon just because they look out of date. I believe implicitly in balance and try to find the sweet spot between tradition and modernity, artefact and nature, art and craft, hand-made and machined.

In what way is your work sustainable?
'Sustainable' is a slippery word; something is really only sustainable if it can be done forever. Bearing that in mind, our core material bamboo can always be planted as fast as it is harvested. The bamboo is actually a secondary resource coming out of forests primarily used for the food production of bamboo shoots. Cutting is done by hand and no machinery is used for moving the poles. Converting the hollow poles into flat sheets relies on a lot of machining and gluing, which is not so good. However, on balance we feel that this is still the best available material to us. We could get a cheaper, similar bass wood plywood, but the virgin forest source is not being replanted.

Our workshop in New Zealand purchases only energy from 100% renewable sources, mostly hydro. We produce virtually no landfill waste, recycling everything we can. We try to prolong the longevity of our products by going for a classic rather than fashionable look so that people aren't encouraged to throw them out too soon.

All our standard lights are kitset for considerable reduction in freight costs (in dollars and environmentally). It has also been proven that people will keep a kitset longer because they have invested themselves in it. In all our lights, we use small amounts of material for maximum effect, using very thin plywood in compound curvature to create a remarkably rigid, lightweight structure.

What materials and techniques do you use?
Most of what we produce uses bamboo plywood. Where light diffusion is required we reluctantly use polycarbonate, but we are developing a PLA (plant-based plastic) mixed with NZ flax fibre to replace this. The small amount of furniture we make uses plantation-grown hoop pine plywood or Eurobeech and sustainably managed American hardwoods.

All the sheet material is cut on a CNC router. Our design technique unrolls complex compound surfaces that are cut out on the flat. When the pieces are 'rolled' back up and reassembled, the form is recreated as a structural skin.

What are you working on at the moment, and what do you hope to work on in the future?
We are currently designing a range of modular acoustic devices for a well-known European company, made from mostly recycled material. We have a number of new ideas for lighting. Earlier this year we launched the Manuka light, which I call a 'constellation light' to distinguish it from the opulent connotations of the word 'chandelier' (see page 130). I am keen to develop this concept further in a range of lighting that also includes wall sconces, something we have so far avoided.

Have you noticed any particular trends in sustainable design?
Obfuscation bothers me a bit. Companies will champion their good points to hide their bad ones. The good news is that they obviously realize the public are starting to value sustainable issues, but the bad news is that they are not telling the full story, hoping that no one will look past their trumpeted achievement. I firmly believe in honesty. We just say we are not certain, but we are doing all we can to improve. Other responsible companies are following a similar course.

What materials or techniques do you think we'll be seeing more of in the future?
We are soon in for a surge of cheap, rapid 3D-prototyping machines as the patents become available. I also think that solid wood is coming back, as is the craft of working it. We will thankfully move away from our globalized model, which ships far too much cheap mass-made stuff all over the place chasing cheap unregulated labour. Instead we will buy more locally, starting to rebuild our communities. So craft will become more valued and with it a connection to local materials through the hand-made. This will result in the products being more responsible: when you see the consequences around you of overusing a resource or a polluting factory, you are more likely to try to prevent it than if it is happening on the other side of the world.

Frankie
Designtree
(Rebecca Asquith &
Tim Wigmore)

FSC-certified silver beech, recycled PET felt
Pendant, H: 35 cm (13¾ in), Diam.: 40 cm (15¾ in)

www.designtree.co.nz

The Frankie lighting series is a tactile and distinctive lighting system, created from a few simple, sustainable components.

The felt material used for the shades consists of 100 per cent recycled and recyclable PET, approximately 60 per cent of which is post-consumer waste. This material has excellent acoustic absorbency, is non-toxic, non-allergenic, highly durable and easy to clean. The silver beech timber used is certified by the FSC for sustainability and can contribute to Green Star ratings.

Each of these lights comes flat-packed for home assembly to reduce its size for transport.

Mikolo
Ekobo

Bamboo, recycled wood
H: 45 cm (17¾ in), W: 20 cm (7⅞ in), D: 15 cm (5⅞ in)

www.ekobohome.com

Mikolo is a table lamp with an adjustable arm made from a recycled wooden coathanger. In keeping with Ekobo's area of specialism, the rest of the lamp is made from bamboo.

Ekobo is an eco-friendly enterprise specializing in the design and manufacture of contemporary home accessories. The company combines modern aesthetics with local craftsmanship to sustain artisanal communities, while promoting bamboo as a socially and environmentally responsible material.

Ekobo trades directly with bamboo-producing villages and small workshops, so artisans receive higher wages, planning is more efficient, and higher-quality standards are maintained. The products are wrapped in recycled paper and cardboard boxes in the village and 98 per cent of these items are shipped by boat rather than by air.

At the end of their life cycle, bamboo products can be composted.

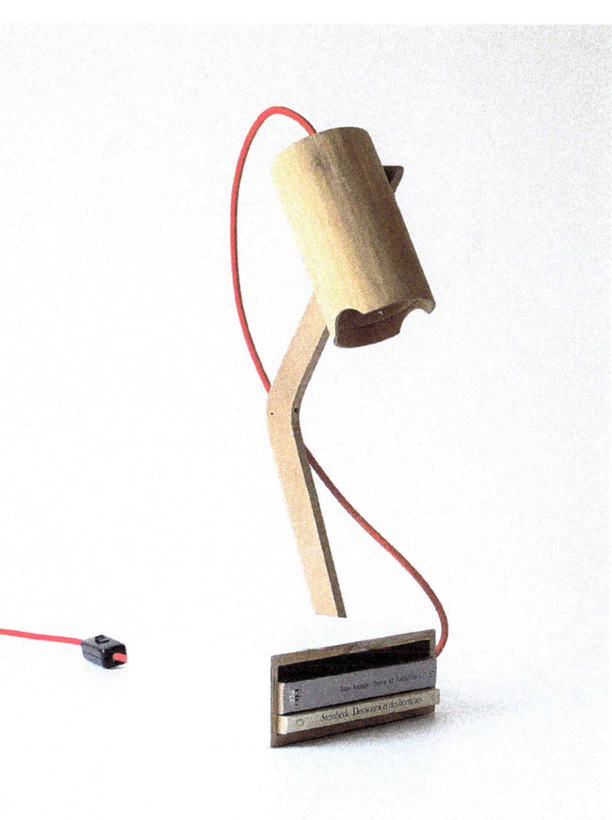

Kami Spin
Ett La Benn
(Oliver Bischoff,
Danilo Dürler &
Johann Gooßen)

Cellulose, paper pulp
H: 30 cm (11¾ in), Diam.: 35 cm (13¾ in)

www.ettlabenn.com

Cellulose is one of the key ingredients in living matter and is found in almost every plant, making it one of the most plentiful natural resources on the planet; unlike many dwindling resources, it is also completely harmless and biodegradable. Ett La Benn's vision is to tap into this abundant material and create a manufacturing process for a series of objects that are both biodegradable and highly sustainable.

The Kami Spin lampshade uses a mix of cellulose and paper pulp, which is given form through industrial rotation moulding. This technique involves using centrifugal forces to uniformly distribute cellulose fibres in a rotating negative mould. The material is then left to air dry before the mould is removed. One advantage of the method is the absence of a joining seam, allowing greater strength in a lampshade with a very thin wall thickness. It also provides a very high quality of surface.

For more on Ett La Benn, see the Q&A on page 138.

Malva
Ett La Benn
(Oliver Bischoff, Danilo Dürler & Johann Gooßen)

Cellulose, viscose
Various sizes

www.ettlabenn.com

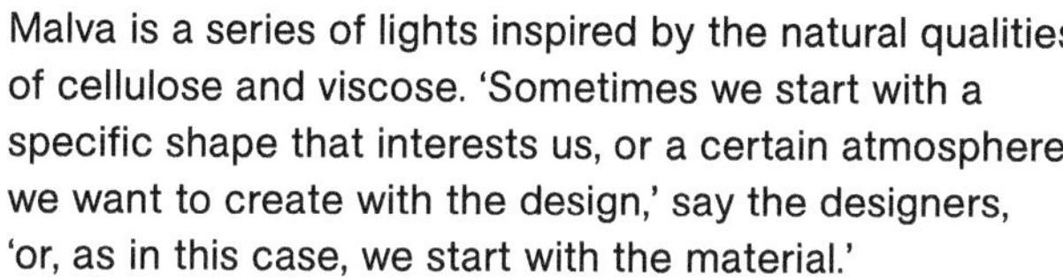

Malva is a series of lights inspired by the natural qualities of cellulose and viscose. 'Sometimes we start with a specific shape that interests us, or a certain atmosphere we want to create with the design,' say the designers, 'or, as in this case, we start with the material.'

The objects are created by draping sponge cloths over positive moulds and dampening them with cellulose, which hardens as it dries out on exposure to air, transforming this everyday material into individual design pieces through basic processes. At the end of its life, the Malva is fully compostable.

Q&A: Ett La Benn

Oliver Bischoff, Danilo Dürler and Johann Gooßen run Berlin-based design agency Ett La Benn. They work across many areas of design, including furniture, lighting, interiors and installations, with a focus on sustainable solutions.

www.ettlabenn.com

Ett La Benn's Bottle Lamps feature old-style bulbs in recycled glass. Leather straps secure power cords.

How would you describe your style?
Modern, experimental, analytical, inspiring, directional, strategic.

In what way is your work sustainable?
We try to build things that are impressive and timeless enough to survive for a long time on the market. Some of our recent lighting projects have been inspired by natural materials, such as cellulose and viscose (see page 136). Cellulose is one of the most abundant natural resources and is completely biodegradable. We are interested not only in designing with sustainable materials, but also designing sustainable manufacturing processes.

What materials and techniques do you use?
Basically anything – whatever is best for each particular project – but we try to instil an overall long-lasting and ongoing influence in everything we do.

What inspires you?
Nothing in particular. Our design focus is the culturally driven lifestyle market, but our processes are quite holistic, so we try to open ourselves to influences from any cultural and social movement.

What are you working on at the moment?
Right now we are working on structures for modern people and contemporary habits –restaurants in Berlin, a special piece for a Vienna-based exclusive perfume company. In the future we plan to develop a holistic food and beverage process.

Have you noticed any particular trends in sustainable design?
We have noticed that while it is important to think about materials and processes, sustainability is much more about the way we use and consume things. We as designers can only give some small suggestions by developing possibilities. The rest is up to all of us!

What materials or techniques do you think we'll be seeing more of in the future?
I think we will see a sustained return to traditional materials – those that have been used for a long time. Naturally grown and not industrially manipulated.

Top: The forms of the Parts range of vessels by Ett La Benn are based on their previous Kami range, made from moulded and air-dried 100% biodegradable cellulose.

Bottom: The multifunctional and space-saving Escritoire Trestle is made from interlocking connecting components.

Connect Series
Facaro (Carolina Fontoura Alzaga)

Metal bicycle components
Various sizes

www.facaro.com

Making the most of the boom in cycling culture and the consequent abundance of damaged and worn-out parts, Facaro's Connect series is a range of chandeliers inspired by both Victorian and contemporary styles, reimagined using recycled bicycle components.

Designer Carolina Alzaga aims to find beauty in the discarded while challenging the necessity of the new. In the Connect series, she carefully combines old bicycle wheels with large amounts of swagged chain, her designs evoking the luxurious, cascading opulence of traditional chandeliers.

Pianissimo
Lars Beller Fjetland
for Discipline

Cork, glass, LEDs
H: 19 cm (7½ in), Diam.: 60 cm (23⅝ in)

www.beller.no
www.discipline.eu

Pianissimo is a pendant lamp made from a strip of toasted cork with a striped surface resembling a piano keyboard. Creating a lampshade from cork would normally require hollowing a large block and creating a lot of waste material. However, the material-conscious design of Pianissimo allows the ribbed cork to flex and wrap around the frosted-glass centre of the lamp. Within this glass shell is a group of low-energy LEDs, providing an efficient glow, softened by the tactile cork shade.

For more on Lars Beller Fjetland, see the Q&A on page 22.

Corola
Emiliano Godoy

FSC-certified plywood, electrical components, metal hardware
Diam.: 150 cm (59 in), D: 60 cm (23⅝ in)

www.emilianogodoy.com

Corola is a large ceiling or wall lamp that comes from a small package, drawing inspiration from a flower's majestic growth from a small bud. To reduce transportation costs and storage space, the lamp ships flat in a box that represents less than 20 per cent of its final size, before being assembled by the end user.

Made from a thin plywood with wood from sustainably managed forests, Corola is machined with a CNC router, then treated with a Livos eco finish. Each of the long arms is cut separately, which allows a very efficient use of the raw material, minimizing waste wood.

The light is provided by efficient, round fluorescent tubes that operate at low temperatures, prolonging the life of the components. However, when the product's life does come to an end, each of the wooden parts can be separated and composted or biodegraded, while the metal components can be recycled.

Save Our Soup
David Graas

Recycled plastic
Small, H: 37 cm (14⅝ in), W: 37 cm (14⅝ in)
Medium, H: 38 cm (15 in), W: 75 cm (29½ in)
Large, H: 75 cm (29½ in), W: 80 cm (31½ in)

www.davidgraas.com

Inspired by the growing amount of discarded plastic in our oceans, Save Our Soup is a pendant light made up of triangular modules composed of recycled plastic soap bottles.

When waste plastic is eaten by small species of marine life, it is slowly but steadily passed up the food chain and will eventually find its way into our own bowls of soup. To prevent this from happening, designer David Graas suggests restricting the use of plastics to durable products that are meant to last, and recycling the material when these products are discarded.

Rather than being used for a disposable product that outlives its purpose, the plastic for this lampshade is saved from our soup and given a new use more fitting for its durability.

Q&A: David Graas

David Graas first became involved in design when he was young, making carts, puppets, puppet theatres, boats, kites and other objects in the workshop at his primary school. After school he studied product design at the Gerrit Rietveld Academie in Amsterdam and discovered that he could turn his childhood passion into a profession. Since 2004 he has worked as an independent product designer.

www.davidgraas.com

Huddle is a 3D-printed bulbshade showing a modern cityscape of close-set high-rises. Directly mounted on the LED bulb that is included, Huddle does not require a separate fixture.

How would you describe your style?

I always start with an idea. Usually an idea about the relationship between people and objects. What makes the objects we use attractive to us, how long lasting is this attraction and how can the design have an influence there? Based on the outcome of the questions I ask, I then try to let the object design itself as much as possible. I like it best when the underlying concept is so well formulated that all the design decisions about material, colour, shape, etc., flow naturally from this concept. The result is something that has some kind of universal logic, which I find very beautiful.

In what way is your work sustainable?

Of course I think about the materials I use, and have things made locally as much as possible – the production side of things. But in the end what makes stuff truly sustainable is how long you can use it and also want to use it. Is the product strong enough to last for many years and will it keep its attraction over the years? Designs that have withstood the test of time often have a very modest appearance, a quietness, a tranquillity maybe, and a familiarity. They look like something you have seen before, even if you haven't. It's this familiarity that I look for when I design – for instance, by using familiar shapes for familiar materials and reinterpreting existing shapes. I found that this familiarity activates an emotional connection between the object and the person using it, raising the chances of an enduring relationship.

What materials and techniques do you use?

I use cardboard for many of my products and I still like this material very much for its total lack of glamour. Lately I have been experimenting with 3D printing. Next to the total freedom in shape you have with this technique, I am fascinated by the logistical possibilities that it brings to product design. Our current industrial model is based on mass-production techniques. In short, the more you make of one thing, the cheaper it gets. Not much attention goes into the quality of a product. With 3D printing and the internet becoming so widespread, I can see a possible shift towards small-scale production of products tailored to the needs and preferences of niche groups. A more humane way of making things, with respect for diversity.

What are you working on at the moment, and what do you hope to work on in the future?

My studio is launching a platform and webshop for 3D-printed products that are produced as locally as possible called layersindesign.com. I'm very curious to see if it's possible to achieve a kind of craftsmanship feel with 3D printing. Not in the sense of material handling, but in the sense of attention to detail and ritual. I think there's a real challenge for designers to translate the possibilities of 3D printing into products with a soul.

Have you noticed any particular trends in sustainable design?

I think the discussion about sustainability is going to move away from the mere production of new products. There is a trend, especially here in densely populated Holland, of people sharing products, instead of everyone buying their own. Why would you want to own a circular saw if you are only going to use it once or twice in your life? What a relief that you don't need all this stuff anymore! Your house will feel so spacy. Just a few items that were custom-made for you and you will love and cherish for many years.

What materials or techniques do you think we'll be seeing more of in the future?

I'm pretty sure 3D printing is going to rock the boat in the coming years. But also small-scale production of handmade items close by, that have a connection with local tradition is something you will see more and more of. There's a genuine need for products with a very personal appeal and the internet facilitates the search for these special items.

Q&A: David Graas

The Lamp Formerly Known as Trombone upcycles a found musical instrument.

Beute Lamp
Herrwolke (Michael Konstantin Wolke)

Corrugated cardboard
H: 30 cm, Diam.: 40 or 60 cm (15¾ or 23⅝ in)

www.herrwolke.com

Michael Wolke's Beute Lamp is made from carefully coiled overlapping strips of corrugated cardboard. The material comes from discarded boxes and embraces all their variations in colour and typographic design, ensuring each piece has a random, unique appearance. The surface of the cardboard is particularly suited to this task and reflects light to create a very warm, ambient glow.

Wolke specializes in creating everyday objects from recycled materials and is conscious and concerned about the rate at which society produces waste. Targeting product packaging as a major contributor to environmental problems, the Beute Lamp saves some of this material from becoming landfill, as well as providing a visual reminder of the impact caused by expensive, unnecessary and harmful waste.

Leather Lamps
Hettler Tüllmann
(Katja Hettler &
Jula Tüllmann)

Recycled leather
Small, H: 33 cm (13 in), W: 33 cm (13 in), D: 33 cm (13 in)
Medium, H: 38 cm (15 in), W: 37 cm (14⅝ in), D: 37 cm (14⅝ in)
Large, H: 30 cm (11¾ in), W: 45 cm (17¾ in), D: 45 cm (17¾ in)

www.hettlertullmann.com

Designer Katja Hettler and architect Jula Tüllmann's Leather Lamps make use of leftover leather scraps, collected from furniture and shoe factories and ground to shreds. These scraps are mixed into pulp with water, natural rubber and acacia wood bark, and are then compressed into sheets and mechanically processed for size, colour and texture.

Each lamp is made by joining six identical geometric pieces cut from one of these flexible sheets. Small holes along the seams allow a glimpse of the interior of the shade and the colourful reverse side of the leather. This unexpected colour also provides a tint to the glow emitted from the lamp.

Copper Lampshade
Pepe Heykoop

Copper, bamboo
H: 30 cm (11¾ in), Diam.: 45 cm (17¾ in)

www.pepeheykoop.nl

Dutch designer Pepe Heykoop's copper and bamboo lampshades are produced in collaboration with the Tiny Miracles Foundation – a Netherlands-based charity that focuses on one specific street in Mumbai's red-light district, India, where a community of around 700 people live right on the pavement. The ambition is to help this group become self-supporting by 2020, with each member of the community enjoying a happy childhood and going on to receive the same education and healthcare as a middle-income worker.

The community's economy traditionally relies on selling cane baskets, but this market is now very small, so Heykoop is training women to make lampshades. Using slices of bamboo lashed together with recycled copper wire cut from electricity cables, the women can take each piece home to work on while running the household at the same time.

Leather Lampshade
Pepe Heykoop

Lambskin leather
Horizontal, H: 34 cm (13⅜ in), W: 83 cm (32⅝ in)
Vertical, H: 72 cm (28⅜ in), W: 62 cm (24⅜ in)

www.pepeheykoop.nl

Although their shapes are inspired by old metal industrial lamps, Pepe Heykoop's Leather Lampshades are made for the domestic environment. Like Heykoop's Copper Lampshades, they are handmade in the workshop set up by Heykoop in collaboration with the Tiny Miracles Foundation in Mumbai. Key to the assembly of the lampshades are 20 mothers living in this community. In addition to creating work for these women, for every lampshade sold, the equivalent of one month's school fees is donated to their daughters.

Heykoop's Leather Lampshades have been manufactured using only animal skins that are a by-product of other industries and are tanned with as many natural materials as possible. The use of leather makes the lampshades lightweight and foldable for ease of shipping.

Float
Benjamin Hubert

Cork
Small, H: 20 cm (7⅞ in), W: 25 cm (9⅞ in), D: 25 cm (9⅞ in)
Medium, H: 30 cm (11¾ in), W: 40 cm (15¾ in), D: 40 cm (15¾ in)
Large, H: 30 cm (11¾ in), W: 52 cm (20½ in), D: 52 cm (20½ in)

www.benjaminhubert.co.uk

Float, by Benjamin Hubert's London design studio, is a pendant lamp made entirely from agglomerate blocks of sustainable Portuguese cork.

Turned by hand using traditional woodworking techniques, the blocks (made using waste from the manufacture of wine stoppers) are simply shaped and hollowed out to create the lamps. Although this process creates a high volume of waste, leftover shavings are fed back into the process and compressed into new blocks of cork for the production of more lamps.

Natural cork is particularly suited to making lamps as it emits a warming glow when illuminated.

Sunnan
IKEA

Steel, polycarbonate plastic, aluminium
H: 44 cm (17⅜ in), Base diam.: 13.5 cm (5⅜ in)

www.ikea.com

⚡ ⚖

Sunnan is IKEA's solar-powered LED table lamp, which generates all of its energy from an integral panel that converts sunlight into electricity. This means it does not require any external cables or plugs, with the result that it can be used almost anywhere. The lamp stores its power in three rechargable AA batteries, guaranteed to last a minimum of two years.

For every Sunnan lamp sold, the IKEA Foundation donates one to UNICEF and Save the Children to help children in India and Pakistan play, read, write and study after dusk; they have donated 700,000 so far. Provision of lamps is particularly important to children in developing countries who struggle to keep up at school because their only opportunity to study is at night after completing household tasks.

Avocetta Lamp
La Quercia 21
(Luca De Pascalis &
Nicola Gubiotti)

Reclaimed wood
H: 70 cm (27½ in), D: 25 cm (9⅞ in), Base diam.: 18 cm (7⅛ in)

www.laquercia21.it

Avocetta is a solid-wood desk lamp, constructed from three different types of reclaimed wood – wenge, maple and walnut, each one maintaining its natural colour. Not only does this provide a contrasting appearance, but each wood is used in accordance with its mechanical strength and weight. The shade, also made entirely of wood, is designed to facilitate the passage of air, and aid cooling of the low-energy halogen bulb.

The finished product is treated with water, beeswax and natural oils.

Moolin
Lasfera

Bamboo
H: 35, 60, 120 or 155 cm (13¾, 23⅝, 47¼ and 61 in)

www.lasfera.de

Moolin lamps are the result of a meeting between modern Beijing, design studio Lasfera and the traditional Chinese craft of heating and bending strips of fresh bamboo.

Like many traditional craft techniques in China, bamboo weaving is in decline. Eventually, however, the designers found the Chen family in a small village near Shenzhen, where the cultivation and processing of a particularly fast-growing, thick-walled bamboo is a tradition. When worked, the bamboo is left unfinished, free of chemical treatments, and can therefore be recycled.

Moolin's design evokes traditional Chinese lanterns, but with clean lines and light colours, which provide a sculptural quality. It also employs the latest energy-saving LED technology.

Quilt Light
Tamara Maynes

Various materials
Any size

www.tamaramaynes.com
www.19greekstreet.com

The Quilt Light does not come as a finished product, but instead is only available as a dowloadable template, to be customized, printed, cut out and decorated by the buyer, who becomes the co-designer.

Conceived by designer and crafter Tamara Maynes, the buyer is able to print the template in any size they wish and create multiple copies of the design in any suitable material, such as wood, cardboard or plastic. Once assembled, the product can be painted, taped and stitched to any specifications before being fitted with the necessary lighting hardware.

SMP Lamp
Sergio Mendoza

Scrap wooden crates
Various sizes

www.sergio-mendoza.com

SMP is a series of lamps created from fragments of salvaged fruit crates combined with timber offcuts. Discovering there was no system in place for recycling wooden crates used at markets all over Spain, designer Sergio Mendoza set out to find simple ways to use this abundance of material, most of which is otherwise burnt.

Mendoza came up with the SMP Lamp, a product that can be made from scratch using very basic materials and techniques in less than an hour.

Maintaining the archetypal shapes of traditional desklights but using completely alien materials, Mendoza has created a series of warm, sympathetic-looking lamps.

Q&A: Sergio Mendoza

Flexibility defines Sergio Mendoza. After studying industrial and product design, Sergio opened his own studio in 2010. Sometimes the company is a product design studio and a collaborative space; sometimes Sergio and his designers are video makers, photographers or design strategists. Sergio's approach to design favours hand techniques and natural materials.

www.sergio-mendoza.com

Mendoza's SMP Lamps are created from disused fruit crates and other scrap materials.

In what way is your work sustainable?
My work is sustainable at a true level. I consider
sustainability a part of the design thinking. It is not only
about the materials but also about common sense
and consciousness of the different realities around the
project. How sustainable is it to use 300 chairs in a
coffee shop that sells coffee for $1? Or how sustainable
is it to design very nice wooden interiors for a business
that cannot economically afford it? Design is a tool that
serves a purpose. We can never forget this.

How would you describe your style?
I have no style! At least not an aesthetic one. I have
collected experiences and learned from others and even
myself. So I guess I have my own way of facing problems
or coming around them.

What materials and techniques do you use?
I like working with my own hands. I am growing more
and more tired of the computer. I enjoy working with
ceramics, wood, cork, even trash (see page 155). My
notebook, screenprinting and cooking are things that
keep me in touch with the real world. I am certainly an
impatient person, so working with my hands means
relying on myself and controlling the timing of whatever
I'm doing. I hate projects that are stuck in bureaucracy or
uncertainty and last forever. I get bored and jump to the
next thing.

**What are you working on at the moment,
and what do you hope to work on in the future?**
I am working on a series of lamps, redoing a little
café and preparing something for Milan Design Week
with the international design collective TIVD (This Is
Very Dangerous).

**Have you noticed any particular trends
in sustainable design?**
Right now, it's obvious that the world of craft is going
through a sweet moment. People are tired of mass
production and soulless objects (and lives). We seriously
have the need to go back to basics, to real life. Wood, not
plastic. I believe we walk into a future where we will have
fewer objects but they will have greater meaning to us.

**What materials or techniques do you think
we'll be seeing more of in the future?**
As we get into this trend of craft, we will see lots of noble
materials: wood, cork, raw metal, glass and even marble.
But at the same time I would also expect an opposing
current: digital, 3D printing, etc. Manmade intelligent
materials have been around for a while and it is time for
them to come into our lives.

The SMP Lamps are designed to
be constructed quickly with basic
materials and techniques.

Repurposed Lighting
MFEO

Various materials
Various sizes

www.wearemfeo.com

MFEO aim to reduce the environmental impact of production by designing products made primarily from salvaged materials and discarded objects. Their range of lighting makes use of a diverse range of repurposed items, from Bakelite telephones and clock radios to skateboard decks and cine film canisters.

Other pieces are made from sections of antique Douglas fir, sourced from the 120-year-old barn in Oregon that once belonged to company co-founder Aaron Van Holland's grandfather.

Clamp Lights
Herminia Mira

Recycled steel
H: 100 cm (39⅜ in), Diam.: 40 cm (15¾ in)

www.herminiamira.com

Herminia Mira's Clamp Lights provide a new purpose for vintage industrial hardware that would otherwise be lying abandoned in derelict Spanish factories. Mira upcycles these forgotten clamps while retaining their original character and function with the addition of simple lighting components to create a practical, portable source of illumination.

Mira regards clippable lights and clamps as everyday nomads, moving around from one place to the next, adding 'One lives in a clean lab-like environment while the other one is always surrounded by concrete and dust. The Clamp Light is a union between these two objects, so different and yet so similar.'

Cloud Softlight
Molo (Stephanie Forsythe & Todd MacAllen)

Recyled paper, textiles, LEDs, FSC-certified hemlock wood
H: 147.3 cm (58 in), Diam.: 56 cm (22 in)

molodesign.com

Stephanie Forsythe and Todd MacAllen's Cloud Softlight is a full-size floor lamp created with a minimum of materials. The shades are made from recycled paper and textiles, with up to 50 per cent recycled content, and their honeycomb design allows for considerable expansion and economy of weight – both important packaging and shipping considerations. The slender legs are made from sustainable hemlock wood, while the illumination is provided by energy-efficient LED lighting, with all electronic components RoHS-certified.

Molo attempts to have an encompassing view of sustainability and believes that products should not only be sustainable themselves, but they should also aid in more sustainable practices in the spaces around them.

Marine Light
Nir Meiri Design Studio

Seaweed, metal
Table lamp, H: 40 cm (15¾ in), Diam.: 33 cm (13 in)

www.nirmeiri.com

Nir Meiri is a designer with an interest in carefully selected, raw and wild materials. These are then shaped into unique clean-cut forms to create unusual products that play on the tension between the domesticated and the untamed.

The Marine Light explores the unconventional use of seaweed as a practical material for the domestic environment. Meiri hopes the introduction of this material into the world of design might inspire new thinking in the field.

The seaweed is hung on a framework of metal strings while still fresh; it shrinks as it dries out to take on the form of the lampshade. It is then coated with a preserving material.

Lamp Invaders
Nonage (Henri Dejeant)

Papier mâché
Various sizes

nonage.fr

Lamp Invaders is a collection of small table lights by French designer Henri Dejeant, crafted in Molding Pulp, a unique formula of bio-plastic made from 90 per cent paper.

Relocating to Morocco, Dejeant learned a range of craft techniques in the souks of his adopted Marrakech before coming up with his own material. This was developed in his workshop using salvaged newspapers, realizing his vision of creating new forms and textures with a supply of recycled and readily available materials.

The finished products are either left in their raw state or coated with an eco-friendly paint.

Gramophone Horn Pendant Light
Original House

Brass, recycled steel
H: 56 cm (22 in), W: 42 cm (16½ in), depending on gramophone

www.original-house.co.uk

This pendant light by reclaimed interiors specialists Original House reuses an antique gramophone horn to create a well-worn and characterful shade.

The brass light fittings and chain are all new, but the horn dates from around 1920, and has the rusting and distressed paint to prove it. However, further deterioration is prevented by a scrub with wire wool and treatment with clear lacquer, fixing the patina in place as well as enriching the colours.

Original House try to help people move away from mass consumerism by offering objects with soul and history, believing that reusing is more efficient than recycling.

Sonne Pendant
Naomi Paul

Cotton cord
Regular, H: 72 cm (28⅜ in), Diam.: 42 cm (16½ in)
XL, H: 100 cm (39⅜ in), Diam.: 60 cm (23⅝ in)

naomipaul.co.uk

Part of the OMI pendant collection, Sonne is a handcrafted, minimal pendant which evolved from designer Naomi Paul's desire to create lighting that is sustainable yet quietly opulent.

Made by hand using traditional crochet techniques, the flat-pack light is constructed from mercerized (waxed) cotton, locally sourced from industry surplus and lit using award-winning Plumen low-energy bulbs. No adhesives are used in its manufacture, and all elements can be easily separated back into their component parts for recycling/reuse, or for a second life as another pendant.

Apollo Pendant Light
Jake Phipps

Coconut fibre, brass
H: 25 cm (9⅞ in), Diam.: 31 cm (12¼ in)

jakephipps.com

Taking its shape from the command modules on the *Apollo* space program, the Apollo light by Jake Phipps is made almost entirely from coconut fibre, a material with enormous environmental and social benefits.

Highly renewable, the coconut fruit grows to full size in just 45 days and the versatile fibre is extracted from its discarded husk. The Apollo's manufacturing process supports cottage industries in Sri Lanka, providing employment from the initial harvesting right through to the lamp's final construction.

Paper Productions
Pia Design
(Pia Wüstenberg)

Paper pulp
Various sizes

www.piadesign.eu

Lighting

A handcrafted light collection made in Ahmedabad, India, Paper Productions is the outcome of a collaborative development project between designer and artisan.

The goal for this light collection was to make very delicate and lightweight structures using the traditional papermaking technique still in use at the Khalamkush Paper Factory. The factory makes its own paper pulp from old cotton rags and is entirely self-sufficient, from the making of the material to the pressing and processing of the finished paper sheets.

Each item in the Paper Productions collection is made by draping and moulding this paper pulp over various objects, such as balloons and funnels, found at the vibrant old market in Ahmedabad. The resulting shapes are wired up and fitted with low-energy LED bulbs.

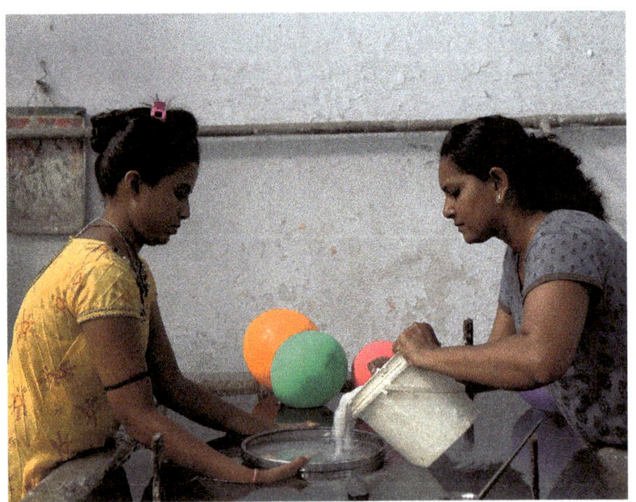

Stratum Lamp
Karim Rashid for Durat

Durat

www.durat.com

Durat is a unique ecological material from Finland that contains about 30 per cent recycled post-industrial plastic (see page 18).

Taking its name from the multicoloured layers, or strata, in a block of Durat, Karim Rashid's Stratum Lamp uses a range of lurid tones to create a design that recalls the bold and sinous shapes of Op Art.

Although the shaping and turning of the lamp creates waste material, Durat is 100 per cent recyclable, so any shavings and dust generated can be reused.

Luna Light
Rawstudio (Nick Rawcliffe)

Metal, LEDs, wire mesh, paper
Various sizes

rawstudio.co.uk

Rawstudio's Luna Light is an ultra-minimal hoop of LED lights, which uses an optical illusion to create an uncanny three-dimensional effect.

The light can be hung either as a simple strip of low-power LEDs, in a metal ring, or with a choice of wire mesh or textured paper to fill the void and provide a lunar surface. When the 10 watts of converging lights shine on the mesh, the resulting interference pattern creates a convincing 3D look. Alternatively, the paper surface, marked by water droplets, provides an organic cratered impression. The paper is made in the Philippines from mulberry, which grows there as a weed.

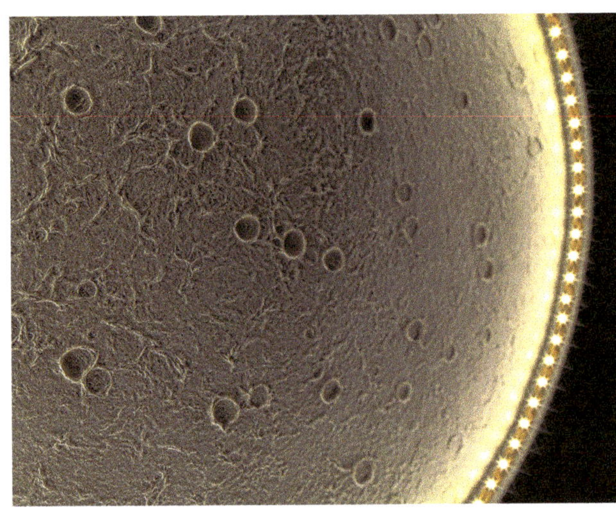

Red Dog Desk Light
The Red Dog
(Philippe Bousquet)

Wood, metal, plastic
Yellow, Base: 12 cm (4¾ in)
Black, Base: 22 cm (8⅝ in)

www.thereddog.co.za

Artist and designer Philippe Bousquet constructs lights from found objects and scrap metal, out of a desire to create beautiful objects without causing harm.

Bousquet began his career as an artist working with precious metals and materials, but after moving to South Africa in 2004, he became increasingly aware of the negative effects of mining on people, communities and the environment. This led him to experiment with a range of waste materials in his Pretoria workshop – mainly wood and plastic – in the hope of breathing new life into items that others have consigned to the dustbin.

Woodrum
Roman and Williams
for Matter

Reclaimed oak, brass
Various sizes

www.romanandwilliams.com
mattermatters.com

Woodrum is a family of lighting – six pieces in all,
including a large chandelier, a sconce, a floor lamp,
a table lamp, a double pendant and a single pendant.

Available in reclaimed white oak with a natural Danish
soap finish, the collection embodies Matter's desire
to create furnishings and fixtures 'whose straightforward
respect for American craft and utility looks to create
something classic and archetypal'. In keeping with the
ethos of both Matter and Roman and Williams, the pieces
are produced in the US by highly skilled craftsmen.

Inspired by obscure 1950s American restaurant lighting
concepts, the robust wood shades follow the tradition
of barrel-stave construction and are turned on a
CNC lathe to achieve the subtle details in form. Hanging
fixtures and the standing lamp utilize a large version
of the shade, while the wall and table lamp are
scaled down.

"

Leaf Lamp
Peter Schumacher for Green Furniture Sweden

FSC-certified birch, unbleached wool felt, unbleached cotton rope
Diam.: 80 or 130 cm (31½ or 51⅛ in)

greenfurniture.se

Allowing nature to dictate its design, Green Furniture's Leaf Lamp consists of a tree trunk and branches made in Swedish birch, wedged together without the use of glue, while the foliage consists of thin, unbleached wool felt leaves. These are left to be attached by the buyer in their own preferred arrangement.

The assembled product is illuminated by a large LED or induction bulb that shines through the foliage to give a soft and natural light. The leaves form a soft labyrinth of several square metres of wool felt with excellent acoustic absorbtion.

Green Furniture aim to be ecologically sound in all aspects of their business, from their products to their everyday activities, and plant a tree for every item of furniture sold.

The Secto Collection
Secto Design (Seppo Koho)

PEFC-certified Finnish birch
Various sizes

www.sectodesign.fi

Secto Design lampshades are created entirely in Finland by highly skilled craftsmen. Designed by architect Seppo Koho, the shades are built to fit low-energy fluorescent bulbs and are made of laminated birch slats, producing a clear and simple Scandinavian feel.

The company pay great attention to environmental friendliness and ecology, including the exclusive use of locally grown PEFC-certified birch. Sawdust created in manufacturing is then compressed into combustible pellets used for heating.

Given that 80 per cent of their lamps are made for export, special attention is given to their packaging materials. These are made from Finnish natural fibre, assembled with cornstarch and non-toxic, water-soluble glue.

Eistla
Stephen Shaheen

Onyx
Various sizes

www.stephenshaheen.com

The Eistla illuminated sculptures by New York-based artist Stephen Shaheen combine high design with low energy consumption. Created from small onyx remnants salvaged from industrial construction, Eistla can be suspended from the ceiling, placed on the floor as a 'stalagmite luminaire', or even used as a table base.

Each design is assembled from offcuts of onyx, cut to a single centimetre in width and laminated together. This allows large volumes to be created while avoiding wastefully carving entire blocks of stone.

The finished pieces are surprisingly lightweight and employ energy-efficient LEDs to emphasize the natural character and beauty of this translucent stone.

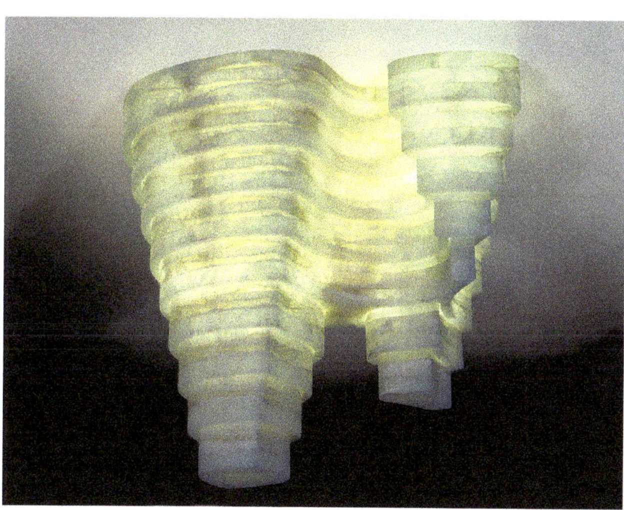

Impasto Lights
Nikolaj Steenfatt

Wood, coffee waste
H: 17.5 cm (7 in), Diam.: 45 cm (17¾ in)

steenfatt.dk

Impasto is a material made from a biodegradable natural fibre composite consisting of animal glues and leftovers from wood and coffee production, invented by Danish designer Nikolaj Steenfatt. The raw materials are mixed with pigment into a dough, then pressed, rolled and folded into flat sheets so that the natural colours become partially mixed, making every batch unique. Afterwards the sheet is moulded to the desired shape by vacuum forming. As well as lights, Steenfatt has also made a coffee table and chairs from the material.

The intention of this graduation project was to create a new material that was biodegradable, easy to work with and adaptable to the industry, but with a unique, 'handmade' appearance.

Better Dog Spotlight
Strand Design
(Ted & Sharon Burdett)

Powder-coated steel, reclaimed old-growth fir
H: 77 cm (30¼ in), W: 27 cm (10⅝ in), D: 38 cm (15 in)

www.stranddesign.org

A reinvention of their Good Dog Spotlight, Strand Design's Better Dog Spotlight has an updated design, which substitutes the original parts with sustainable materials. The body is made from reclaimed old-growth fir, locally sourced in urban Chicago, while the remainder is cast in locally fabricated steel. The lamp even has locally sourced electrical components and is entirely made – from design to assembly – by hand in Chicago.

"

Flip Flop Lamps
Studio Schneemann
(Diederik Schneemann)

Recycled flip flops
Various sizes

www.studioschneemann.com

Hoping to create awareness through playfulness rather than a slap on the wrist, 'A Flip Flop Story' is a colourful collection of products by Rotterdam-based Studio Schneemann, made from the thousands of pairs of abandoned flip flops washed up on the beaches of Kenya and Senegal, where they are found and collected.

The footwear is then transformed into new products in local workshops where, in cooperation with Studio Schneemann, several models are manufactured, providing a living for a number of local workers.

Plastic Bag Light
Supercyclers &
Blakebrough + King

Plastic bag, LEDs, steel wire
H: 30 cm (11¾ in), Diam.: 27 cm (10⅝ in)

supercyclers.com
blakebroughking.com
www.19greekstreet.com

Supercyclers Sarah King and Liane Rossler and their collaborators Blakebrough + King aspire to highlight the innovative ways in which waste material can be transformed into beautiful, functional and meaningful products, and try to inspire the public to upcycle waste into their own design objects. King and Rossler started Supercyclers in order 'to look at using waste creatively and immediately [and] encourage others to have some fun doing it' (see page 29).

Proving that nothing is too lowly for their attention, the Plastic Bag Light gives a modest, single-use bag a new life as a lampshade. Reminiscent of a hot air balloon, its archetypal globe-shaped form is illuminated by a simple low-energy LED light source.

FANtasized
Sep Verboom

Recycled fans
Various sizes

www.fantasized.eu

Accepting the challenge of a local councillor to create a new product out of waste materials in Cebu, the Philippines, Belgian product designer Sep Verboom began a five-month residency, living and working with local people. This exchange led to the creation of the FANtasized lamp, a product which recycles defunct electric fan components and waste plastic strips from a chair factory, while taking advantage of Cebu's highly regarded weaving industry.

FANtasized aims to create environmental awareness, while also providing a livelihood for Cebu's craftspeople. Verboom accepts that while the project will not solve all their problems, it nevertheless emphasizes 'the importance of a responsible cooperative design approach'.

HW Timber Anglepoise
Henry Wilson

Wood, recycled metal
H: 80 cm (31½ in), W: 20 cm (7⅞ in), D: 20 cm (7⅞ in)

henrywilson.com.au
www.19greekstreet.com

Designer Henry Wilson's anglepoise is an update of the classic anglepoise lamp, incorporating modern technology and select handcrafted components. The lamp has been rewired to accomodate an almost invisible low-power LED light source, emphasizing the intricate engineering and restraint of the original design.

According to Wilson, the lamp is 'a statement about the production of entirely new objects for an already saturated world. There is already so much around for us to admire and work from. By applying new thought, time and material to an object already firmly perceived to be a classic, we are forced to consider it in a new way.'

A4Adesign · Christa Badenhorst · Bally
Humanufactured · Bambu · Bee's Wrap · Benwu
Studio · Tord Boontje & Emma Woffenden ·
Arian Brekveld · Bril · Fernando & Humberto
Campana · Charcoal People · Chelsea Miller
Knives · Sebastian Cox · Qiyun Deng · Design Soil ·
Ella Doran · EcoForms · Piet Hein Eek · Ekobo ·
Esque Studio · Ett La Benn · Filles du Facteur ·
Lars Beller Fjetland · Ryan Frank · Grain · Green &
Associates · Green Furniture Sweden · Ineke Hans ·
Hendzel + Hunt · Pepe Heykoop · Gemma Holt ·
Jesse Howard & Thomas Lomée · Ruben Iglesias ·
Cordula Kehrer · La Quercia 21 · Eleanor Lakelin ·
Lanzavecchia + Wai · Hannah Lobley · Loll Designs ·
Loowatt · Madwa · Michela Milani · Mumo ·
Nanimarquina · Nendo · Node · Nudie Jeans ·
Roger Oates · Oxgut Hose Co. · Oyyo · People
of the Sun · Place de Bleu · Catarina Riccabona ·
RushMatters · Salamanca Design · Serpent Sea ·
Siyazama Project · Studio Formafantasma · Studio
Libertíny · Studio Noam Dover · tado° · Utopia and
Utility · Mark Vaarwerk · Marjan van Aubel · Kirstie
van Noort · Vert Design · Debbie Wijskamp ·
Tim Willey · Wonderbag · Zuperzozial

Home Accessories

Cardboard Animals
A4Adesign

Cardboard
Various sizes

www.a4adesign.it

These flat-pack animals are just a small sample of A4A's wide range of designs in recycled, recyclable cardboard. This Italian company specializes in both simple and high-tech products, from toys and accessories to furniture and even stage sets.

Although cardboard lends itself to temporary uses, owing to its low cost, it can also be made flame-retardant and water-repellent, creating a more durable material with useful qualities. For those who appreciate its aesthetic, cardboard is a cheap, lightweight, flexible, sustainable and highly versatile resource.

For more on A4Adesign, see the Q&A on page 36.

Smeul
Christa Badenhorst

Recycled textiles
Various sizes

bchrista.com

Smeul, a collection of recycled textile vessels, is the result of Christa Badenhorst's exploration into new and uncharted ways of creating textile artworks and designer craft pieces from unwanted waste materials.

Created using stitch construction processes, the vessels are made from recycled fabrics that have been sorted, washed, fragmented and layered over a three-dimensional paper and fabric mâché structure.

D.P.W Platters
Bally Humanufactured
(Boris Bally)

Recycled aluminium, copper rivets
Various sizes

www.borisbally.com

Pressed from obsolete aluminium street signs, Boris Bally's 'traffic graphic' platters provide consumers with a contemporary design, hewn from a piece of raw American culture.

Bally is an artist and metalsmith who believes the bold colours and iconic symbols of street signs are ideally suited to creating striking designs through pressing, forming and riveting them into bowls. With discarded signs chosen for their thickness, condition and graphics, no two platters are exactly alike.

Lacquerware
Bambu

Bamboo, lacquer, paper
Various sizes

www.bambuhome.com

Bambu's Lacquerware is made from certified organic coiled bamboo, shaped by hand, coated with multiple layers of a food-safe lacquer from the cashew nut tree, then finished with an even more durable food-safe lacquer.

Manufactured in Vietnam, each piece is entirely handmade by artisans whom Bambu provide with a number of benefits, including higher-than-average wages, housing subsidies, unemployment benefits and medical cover.

Bambu's commitment to sustainability also extends to the packaging, which uses vegetable oil-based inks and FSC-certified paper.

For more on Bambu, see the Q&A on page 186.

Q&A: Bambu

A desire to turn people on to renewable materials and lessen the impact we have on the earth's limited natural resources inspired husband-and-wife team Jeffrey Delkin and Rachel Speth to leave their corporate management positions, move from Portland, Oregon, to China and start Bambu. Now they work to create handcrafted products from local materials in a way that supports sustainable business practices.

www.bambuhome.com

Bambu utensils are hand shaped from a single piece of certified organic bamboo.

How would you describe your style?

Design first. To design simplicity and functionality into our designs to promote more sustainable living. We find inspiration in daily-use objects. We look at the world around us, ask ourselves a lot of questions. Where can we bring elements of functionality and innovation? It is not enough to be eco-friendly. It has to have an aesthetic quality too.

In what way is your work sustainable?

The word 'sustainable' takes on different meanings to different people. We like this simple term. Enduring. This informs our product process, our relationships, and the notion that 'there is no away'. How do we create an enduring supply chain? In our use of renewable materials. But also in improving our waste streams. Where can we eliminate waste? Or more often we ask: What can we create from the waste this is created? Our bamboo Pebbles are a great example of that, made from leftover edges and pieces that are often discarded and burned. Our coconut bowls are another example. Coconut shells are usually discarded and burned after the meat is harvested. We asked: Can we create something beautiful from the waste?

We subscribe to the idea that 'it's more than a product'. Sustainable design is about the choices you make. It is about the packing material we use. Or the glues we don't use, or the inks we use, the alternative methods of transportation, the paper we select, our choice to use non-animal products.

What materials and techniques do you use?

We have our own production workshop so we do a lot of prototyping. We experiment and explore with different materials. Even though our name is Bambu, we always intended to branch out and innovate and design with numerous renewable, reclaimed and recycled materials.

We are really enjoying working with cork fabric. It is a beautiful, versatile material that gets better with age. We will continue to find new and wonderful uses for bamboo, which has so much versatility. We designed a basket made from sedge grass, a scrub grass grown on unproductive soil in central Vietnam. We are creating new products made with hemp. And there's more on the list!

Have you noticed any particular trends in sustainable design?

There is a groundswell of creative thinking in sustainable design, from our homes to our food sources, transportation and cities. That's exciting. But there is another side too: the opportunistic, unauthentic, 'green-washing' that too many companies are engaged in to try to capitalize on the trend. We are excited with the current DIY trend. The notion of makers is one that reflects more people getting back in touch with materials and source of origin.

What materials or techniques do you think we'll be seeing more of in the future?

Waste = beauty. Waste = value. Or waste is eliminated entirely. DIY will continue to grow as people look to form connections, not only digitally but with the natural world. We are at the stage where we are rethinking our whole way of making and consuming. We've got to make dramatic changes in the way we live.

The utensils are made without glues or adhesives, and are finished with an organic food-safe oil.

Bee's Wrap
Bee's Wrap (Sarah Kaeck)

Cotton, beeswax, tree resin, jojoba oil
Small, 17.8 × 20.3 cm (7 × 8 in)
Medium, 25.4 × 28 cm (10 × 11 in)
Large, 33 × 35.6 cm (13 × 14 in)
Bread wrap, 43.2 × 58.4 cm (17 × 23 in)

www.beeswrap.com

Bee's Wrap is an innovative, multifunctional wax-coated cloth for preserving foods, intended as an eco-friendly alternative to plastic bags and wraps. Creator Sarah Kaeck found that by treating pieces of calico (muslin), flour sacks and scraps of trimmings with natural beeswax, jojoba oil and tree resin, she was able to create a pleasing and practical means of food storage.

The antibacterial properties of beeswax and jojoba oil make Bee's Wrap easy to clean, help keep food fresh, and allow the wrap to be used again and again, before eventually being composted.

Living Material Kitchenware
Benwu Studio (Peng You & Hongchao Wang)

Jesmonite, wood
Various sizes

www.benwustudio.com

These kitchen items were created by Peng You and Hongchao Wang of Benwu Studio as part of their unique Living Material project (see page 12). This concept involved embedding twigs and branches in blocks of coloured jesmonite to create an ultra-modern material with rustic roots that celebrates the beauty of everyday nature.

When the blocks are machined into geometric multifaceted objects, the twigs are cut open and exposed to create a distinctive contrasted effect.

tranSglass
Tord Boontje & Emma Woffenden for Artecnica

Glass bottles
Various sizes

tordboontje.com
www.artecnicainc.com

A simple example of upcycling, the idea behind tranSglass is to take an empty bottle and recycle it into an enduring and desirable object.

A diagonally cut Soave bottle becomes a jug, two Chardonnay bottles make a carafe. A Silician table wine bottle transforms into a vase for orchids, and the bottoms of beer bottles make a group of drinking glasses.

With the help of Aid to Artisans, a non-profit organization providing assistance to artisans worldwide, Artecnica collaborates with Guatemalan craftsmen to manufacture tranSglass in a newly created workshop, where young people learn the skills of glassmaking.

Bat Trang Collection
Arian Brekveld for Imperfect Design

Ceramic
Various sizes

www.arianbrekveld.com
imperfectdesign.nl

Specializing in handcrafted lifestyle products, Imperfect Design invite renowned Dutch designers to travel to developing countries and emerging markets to work in close collaboration with local artisans. The Bat Trang ceramics collection is the result of a collaboration between designer Arian Brekveld and Vietnamese ceramicist Mr Nguyen, matching modern European design with traditional Asian handcrafts.

During a research trip to Vietnam in 2012, Brekveld was struck by the unusual local ceramic products made of colored clay. The Bat Trang collection combines this coloured clay with enamel, resulting in a vibrant range of vases and matching plates.

Hanoi Fabrics
Arian Brekveld for Imperfect Design

Wool, hemp
W: 140 cm (55⅛ in)

www.arianbrekveld.com
imperfectdesign.nl

The Hanoi Fabrics collection is a range of plaids and cushions made by Arian Brekveld in collaboration with craftswomen from the Vietnamese countryside, who combine their embroidery with life as farmers.

Inspired by the variety of materials, possible techniques and the craftsmanship he encountered on his research trip to Vietnam, Brekveld decided to embrace an unusual combination of materials and colours. While one side of each cushion has the warmth and comfort of soft wool, the other is of silk, embellished with hand-embroidered stitch patterns. Then, as a neat perk of the women also keeping livestock, they are finished with buttons made of discarded animal horn.

Saigon Lacquer
Arian Brekveld for Imperfect Design

Wood, cashew laquer
Various sizes

www.arianbrekveld.com
imperfectdesign.nl

The Saigon Lacquer collection brings together the contemporary Dutch design aesthetic of Arian Brekveld with the expertise of Vietnamese master craftsman Mr Niên and his colleagues.

The collection includes two low tables, serving trays and candle holders, created using several layers of wood to build up the basic, geometric form of each piece; 16 layers of cashew lacquer are then applied in the traditional Vietnamese fashion, resulting in beautifully finished products without seams. This method results in unique products that cannot be emulated using any other process.

transNeomatic
Fernando & Humberto Campana for Artecnica

Scooter tyre, wicker
H: 7.5 cm (3 in), Diam.: 57 cm (22½ in)
H: 10 cm (3⅞ in), Diam.: 42 cm (16½ in)

campanas.com.br
www.artecnicainc.com

This container bowl is crafted from a repurposed scooter tyre and natural wicker, packaged in a reusable drawstring tote. Each tyre is thoroughly steam-cleaned and finished in an eco-friendly sealant. The bowl also comes with an optional handwoven hemp cover that slips over its rubber base.

The transNeomatic bowl is designed by Estudio Campana and handcrafted by skilled artisans in rural Vietnam. Through Vietnamese non-profit organization Craft Link, Artecnica collaborated with Hai Tai rattan weavers and Hmong women weavers to create each piece. Disadvantaged young Vietnamese were also enlisted to assemble the totes, providing them with artisan training and a framework for establishing sustainable livelihoods.

Bamboo Charcoal Water Filters
Charcoal People

Bamboo charcoal
L: 5 cm (2 in)

www.charcoalpeople.co.uk

Made in traditional clay kilns in Japan, bamboo charcoal provides a simple and natural way of filtering tap water. Left in a jug of water it works like a sponge, slowly filtering out impurities such as chlorine while releasing beneficial minerals.

Bamboo charcoal's incredible filtering ability comes from its super-porous structure – 1 g (0.04 oz) of high-quality bamboo charcoal has a surface area equivalent of up to three tennis courts.

Charcoal water filtering leaves no waste and is produced from sustainable materials without chemical processes.

Knives
Chelsea Miller Knives

High-carbon steel, wood
Various sizes

www.chelseamillerknives.com
www.madesmith.com

American Chelsea Miller cuts her knives from discarded high-carbon steel horseshoe rasps once used by Vermont farriers. True to their origins, the blades retain these cross-cut file patterns, while the edge is laboriously ground down and sanded until smooth and sharp.

The wooden handles are crafted from apple, spalted maple and cherry, chosen for their unique grain patterns from scrap piles on Miller's childhood farm in Vermont. The entire making process for each beautiful handcrafted knife can take up to two days to complete.

For more on Chelsea Miller, see the Q&A on page 198.

Lop & Top Candelabra
Sebastian Cox

Coppiced hazel
L: 30 cm (11¾ in), W: 11 cm (4⅜ in), H: 20 cm (7⅞ in)

sebastiancox.co.uk

Created by Sebastian Cox from sustainable hazel, harvested in Lincolnshire, England, this rustic woodland candelabra makes use of the parts of the hazel rods that are not straight enough for chair legs or table rails.

Working exclusively with hazel and other English hardwoods, Cox is playing a part in reviving the British timber industry, supporting well-managed coppices (see pages 52, 127).

For more on Sebastian Cox, see the Q&A on page 128.

Q&A: Chelsea Miller

Chelsea Miller started making knives in her father's blacksmith shop after having seen a knife her brother had made. Her knives are created by hand from repurposed high-carbon steel from discarded tools, with handles of local maple, cherry and applewood from her family's farm in Vermont.

www.chelseamillerknives.com

One-of-a-kind cheese or butter knife, crafted from found materials on her family's farm in Vermont.

How would you describe your style?
My style is nontraditional, inspired by materials that
are not typically used for things beyond their original
purpose. I am excited by textures and grain and letting
each piece find its final form.

How is your work sustainable?
My work is sustainable in the sense that I am repurposing
old farm and farriers' tools and milling wood from the
living forest where I grew up. It's fun to imagine someone
cutting and cooking with what once was a file used
to shoe horses, when otherwise they would have never
come in contact with such a tool.

What tools and materials do you use?
I use high-carbon-steel tools, all made in the USA, and
wood native to my childhood home in the North East
Kingdom of Vermont. I cut the desired shape from
these tools with a torch, then grind them to the optimal
thinness. I heat-treat and temper the blades, attach
wood handles, and many, many hours later chop veggies
and grate cheese.

What inspires you?
My inspiration comes from a need for balance in my
life. I live in New York City, and I occasionally act in films;
knife making gives me the meditative time I need to
focus all my energy on creating something very simple
in theory yet quite complex in reality.

I am also intrigued by creative thinking in music and
sustainability, handmade goods that are typically mass-
produced, and above all, children. I will always be inspired
by children and their power to create an imaginary
world. I try to spend a lot of time there.

File patterns on Miller's knives
reveal the steel blades' previous
life as horseshoe rasps.

Graft
Qiyun Deng

Polylactic acid
Various sizes

cargocollective.com/qiyun

Graft is a series of disposable tableware items made of polylactic acid (PLA), a compostable bio-plastic derived from renewable plant sources. The collection was the outcome of Qiyun Deng's four-month master's degree project at ECAL, Switzerland.

Given that these products are made from fruits and vegetables, Deng reasoned that moulding them in the form of their ingredients would be the perfect way to subtly introduce bio-plastics and raise awareness of sustainability.

The collection aims to change attitudes towards cheap, disposable products, hoping that by making them more tactile and desirable, consumers will be reluctant to throw them away so readily.

Fadeless
Design Soil (Nobu Miake)

Brass, wood, leather strap, rubber band
Various sizes

www.designsoil.jp

Fadeless, by Nobu Miake of the Design Soil project, is an extension of the Japanese concept of *ichirinzashi*, or the single-flower vase. This series of pieces is designed to prolong the life of that one important stem by slowly drying it out upside down, then turning it back around to be displayed indefinitely.

These minimal vases evoke a tradition inspired by a historic reverence for nature and simplicity. By replacing large, temporary bouquets with a permanent single stem, Fadeless provides an alternative to the cut-flower industry and its dependency on chemicals, energy and transportation.

Natural Collection
Ella Doran for WovenGround

Kesav, okra, rati, makai, hyacinth, jute
Various sizes

www.wovenground.com

A reflection of Ella Doran's interest in natural structures and geometric shapes, this collection of rugs by WovenGround provides a range of flooring using a variety of ecologically produced fibres from sustainable sources. The materials are harvested and dried before being hand-plaited into a fishbone pattern and tied with hand-sewn jute at both ends.

Some of the fibres used, such as kesav and okra, are traditionally used in rope making, while makai leaves are actually a discarded by-product of the plant's booming role in bio-fuel production. Aquatic hyacinth plants not only provide a tough and flexible material but are also highly suited to wastewater treatment, as they tolerate high levels of pollution.

What they all have in common, though, is that they are some of the softest, smoothest underfoot fibres of all natural floor coverings. They are also very strong, durable and easy to clean – unlike sisal, which stains easily, or grass reed, which needs regular watering.

Durat Sink
Durat

Polyester plastic
Various sizes

www.durat.com

Durat sinks are made in Finland from moulded Durat, a unique and versatile polyester-based material (see page 18). Durat contains about 30 per cent recycled post-industrial plastic, granulated into tiny pieces, which is what gives these sinks their distinctive speckled appearance.

The raw material is made in a range of more than 70 colours, and using flexible moulds, so the sinks can be cast in a limitless variety of bespoke sizes. Durat is particularly suited to the manufacturing of sinks as the smooth, seamless finish is very hygienic and can even be renewed by light sanding.

Nova Series
EcoForms

Rice hulls, natural binding agents, organic pigments
Various sizes

ecoforms.com

Nova plant pots are made from rice hulls and natural binding agents, which are starch-based, water-soluble and biodegradable. No pollutants are used or produced at any stage of the manufacturing process. And, because all scraps are recycled in the production process, no materials are wasted. Only a small amount of water is used in the binding formula, and the organic pigments are environmentally friendly. Heat and pressure bind the ingredients to produce the pots.

EcoForms is a family-founded business that grew out of the desire to find a resilient, yet compostable alternative to plastic plant pots. The result is an extensive line of biodegradable pots derived from renewable grain fibres, designed to support sustainable gardening practices and reduce reliance on petroleum-based products. The company also operates from a solar-powered factory, with local delivery trucks running on 100 per cent bio-diesel.

Fat Ceramics
Piet Hein Eek for FairForward

Ceramic
Various sizes

fairforward.nl

Ceramics manufacturers in Thailand tend to aim for the thinnest, finest possible ceramics in response to the current demands of the Western market. However, creating these designs is not easy and often means using porcelain, which is extremely inefficient to produce and has a very high firing temperature.

The Fat ceramics collection is Dutch designer Piet Hein Eek's pragmatic response to this situation – a fairtrade project, produced in colloboration with the Sang Arun company. The designs are unashamedly tactile and chunky, and much easier to produce. Being made from local clay, fired at low temperatures, they are inherently more sustainable.

For more on Piet Hein Eek, see the Q&A on page 58.

Palm Wood Collection
Piet Hein Eek for FairForward

Palm wood
Various sizes

fairforward.nl

This collection of baskets, bowls and trays by Piet Hein Eek for FairForward is made in Vietnam from rejected palm-wood breadboards. Palm wood is difficult to work with as it warps easily, which can lead to a surplus of waste boards. However, by chopping these into strips and joining them with thread (using knots learnt from local fishermen), Eek gives these boards new life and a new purpose.

The pieces are made in a family-owned workshop by a team of 300 craftspeople who belong to an association called Mai Vietnamese Handicrafts. Thirty per cent of the proceeds from the designs are donated to scholarships for Vietnamese students.

For more on Piet Hein Eek, see the Q&A on page 58.

Biobu
Ekobo

Bamboo
Various sizes

www.ekobohome.com

Focusing on pairing modern aesthetics with local bamboo and lacquer handcraft, French home accessories brand Ekobo aim to offer a practical and realistic alternative to plastic, melamine or disposable dinnerware.

Ekobo choose to work with bamboo because it is one of the earth's most abundant renewable resources. It is fast-growing, naturally regenerative and flourishes organically without pesticides, fertilizers or herbicides. It can also be harvested every three years without damaging the plant or the surrounding environment.

The Biobu range is designed for children and intended for daily use at home or outdoors. It is made from a natural resin of bamboo fibre mixed with plant cellulose and is completely biodegradable.

Beer Bottle Bottles
Esque Studio (Andi Kovel & Justin Parker)

Glass, gold leaf
340 or 680 ml (12 or 24 oz)

shop.esque-studio.com

Beer Bottle Bottles are a collection of 250 bottles and vases by Brooklyn-based design studio Esque. Each item is created from a recycled beer bottle, melted in a low-energy electric furnace that runs on wind power. The bottles are distorted, stretched and transformed through intense heat to create a new shape, while leftover glass from the melt is reformed and used again to create further hand-blown beer bottles. Once reformed and cooled, the original product labels are then reimagined with gold leaf, for a final upcycled touch.

For more on Esque Studio, see the Q&A on page 210.

Kami Pots
Ett La Benn
(Oliver Bischoff, Danilo Dürler & Johann Gooßen)

Cellulose
Various sizes

www.ettlabenn.com

The Kami collection of pots and vases by Ett La Benn aims to encourage a new perception of eco-friendliness and reconsideration of design materials. Although the pieces have a matt grey surface like concrete, they are in fact made from 100 per cent biodegradable cellulose, which can be shaped by hand on a potter's wheel before being left to air dry.

Cellulose has great potential as a raw material for sustainable design as it is hugely abundant in nature. It is also very strong and, unlike concrete, extremely light.

For more on Ett La Benn, see the Q&A on page 138.

Q&A: Esque Studio

Based in Portland, Oregon, Esque Studio is a collaboration between glassmakers Andi Kovel and Justin Parker. They create glass works that toe the line between fine art and craft and function. The studio was included in the 'Green' category of *Time* magazine's Style and Design 100.

www.shop.esque-studio.com

Esque Studio's Salt Bombs are designed to hold and pour ground spices. Glass is 'hot gathered' and pulled to points, which are then ground flat and polished, with one spout left for pouring.

How would you describe your style?

Odd. Reserve. Emotion based. Sincere. With Esque we're a bit smirky and playful, even when we're being serious. Our goal is to strip away the pretensions associated with a material, throwing out the questions 'Is it craft?', 'Is it design?' Isn't it obvious? It's both. It's neither. We are breaking glass away from the notion of craft and kitsch, away from the pedestal. We want our glass to be used and handled, to belong in modern settings, to inspire thought and ideas about subjects larger than itself. Nothing is off limits in our creations, as long as they are rooted in content and concept. This is our jumping-off point. Colour and form are the end product, not the starting point.

In what way is your work sustainable?

Esque's new studio was built with a conscience. Using cutting-edge technology to reduce waste and gas consumption, we built two wind-powered electric furnaces that run three to four times more efficiently than traditional gas furnaces. Each day, approximately 45kg (100lb) of excess glass is reused to produce our Eco line, the Delano Esque line and a new line of 100% recycled, chemical-free products. We also pack our glass in biodegradable peanuts and 50% of materials are reclaimed. The quality of our work hasn't changed, but our methods have.

What materials and techniques do you use?

We blow soft glass, using traditional Italian and Swedish techniques. Our tools are the same forged metal tools used for hundreds of years. We also use fruit wood, wet newspaper, plaster moulds, graphite and a steel table to form the glass.

Justin and I both work from different inspirations at the start of piece. I always start from a sketch. I have countless notebooks filled with completed ideas and future works. Justin creates from the material itself. He designs with the glass in hand. Justin loves to play with optical qualities and distortions; I love to impose sculptural forms and conceptual meaning into my pieces. Glass to me exists as its own material. It is one of the oldest art forms, and is steeped in tradition. Most glass artists get so caught up in me 'right way' to make something, that they completely sever themselves from that moment of creation. From a unique act.

What are you working on at the moment, and what do you hope to work on in the future?

This past year has definitely been our most accomplished. We just started working with Design Within Reach, which I'm very excited about. Not because they have a large number of showrooms, but because all of their designers are iconic and their designs timeless. It's amazing to be grouped with such visionaries as Isamu Noguchi, Eero Saarinen and Ludwig Mies van der Rohe. We just shipped a lighting installation to the W Hotel, and one to Hugo Boss in New York. We love the kind of luxury they epitomize and love seeing our work paired with architecture – the glass seems to evoke an emotional response to such spaces. I really enjoy designing. I hope to have the opportunity in the future to design for other companies, in other materials.

Have you noticed any particular trends in sustainable design?

As far as trends in sustainable design, it's just really nice to see that it has moved beyond a trend and into a lifestyle choice; in the near future it won't even have to be a choice, but will be a given. Sustainable materials are now easily accessible and have moved away from a hippie aesthetic, and now embody all types of taste levels and price points.

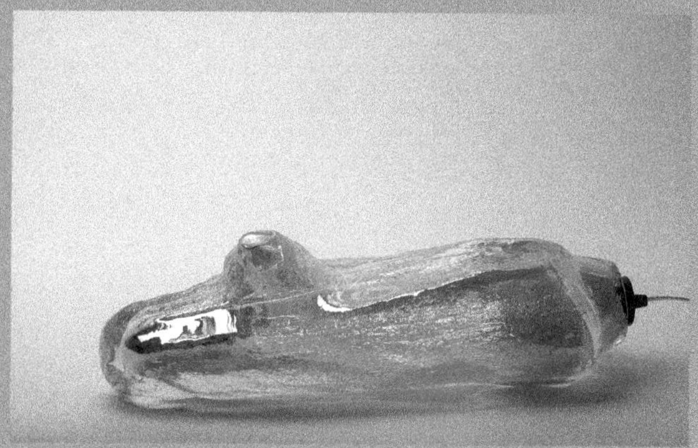

Molten glass is blown into a rotten tree stump to capture the realistic texture found in the Log Light.

Baskets
Filles du Facteur

Recycled plastic bags
Various sizes

www.fillesdufacteur.com

Filles du Facteur's intricate, patterned baskets are woven in Burkina Faso from plastic bags, providing income to local women trained in crocheting techniques. The French company collects plastics for recycling to raise awareness of plastic waste and its effect on the environment. They even send coloured bags from Europe to supplement the endless supply of black bags that proliferate in Africa.

Filles du Facteur's goal is to help women in difficulty, with priority being given to immigrant women in France and women in rural areas of Africa. The aim is to help them help themselves by providing them with work so they can achieve financial independence and access to health and education.

Re-turned
Lars Beller Fjetland
for Discipline

100% recycled wood
Various sizes

www.beller.no
www.discipline.eu

Re-turned is an ever-growing family of wooden birds, made entirely from pieces of recycled timber. The birds are the result of Norwegian designer Lars Beller Fjetland's desire to 'elevate leftover wood from being merely an ignored piece of trash, to becoming a desired piece of feel-good woodcraft'.

'Perhaps they were once part of a loving household as a supportive table leg or an armrest,' says Fjetland. 'Perhaps they never made it from their roots in the woods and into a finished piece of furniture, but got cut off somewhere along the way.' Either way, after being turned on a lathe and fitted with eyes and beaks they are given a new shot at life as a Re-turned bird.

For more on Lars Beller Fjetland, see the Q&A on page 22.

Grapple
Ryan Frank with Biowert Industrie

AgriPlast, linen webbing
H: 16.5 cm (6⅛ in), W: 10 cm (3⅞ in), D: 2.5 cm (1 in)

www.ryanfrank.net

Inspired by industrial crane hooks, Grapple is a hanging system for coats, hats and bags fabricated from natural jute webbing and an innovative composite material called AgriPlast.

Intended as an alternative to petroleum-based plastic, AgriPlast is made from a small percentage of recycled plastic and meadow grass clippings. The material has been developed by German company Biowert, a refining plant that processes grass into environmentally friendly bio-plastics, insulation and green electricity.

The final result is a 100-per-cent-recyclable strong and natural bio-plastic with the faintest smell of meadow.

Bamboo Twist
Nicole Goymann for Juli Hara

Bamboo paper
H: 400 cm (157½ in), W: 100 cm (39⅜ in)

www.julihara.net

Bamboo Twist is a carpet/wall covering designed by Nicole Goymann, which deconstructs the traditional crafts of Hangzhou in China and applies them to contemporary design.

With a background in dressmaking and the textiles industry, Goymann is now focused on interior design products, although the elaborate cutting, manipulation and weaving of bamboo paper in this piece is a natural transition from her past experience.

While bamboo as a raw material is known for its strength and flexibility, when converted into paper it becomes quite fragile. It is thin, the fibre is short, and it can be torn very easily. It seems as though all the physical properties of bamboo disappear during the process of papermaking. However, because the paper in Bamboo Twist is twisted and woven together so tightly, the strength and flexibility of the original material reappear, creating a practical and durable product.

Comalapa
Grain (James &
Chelsea Minola)

Wool, hemp
H: 50.8 cm (20 in), W: 50.8 cm (20 in), D: 14 cm (5½ in)

www.graindesign.com

Grain is dedicated to social and environmental responsibility. Their work combines modern manufacturing technology and age-old craft techniques to create small editions of products as sustainably as possible. This takes place either in their island studio near Seattle, or in Guatemalan artisan communities.

Before bringing anything new to market, Grain carefully consider how their design improves upon an existing product or solves a problem. Their goal is 'not just to do less bad, but to create opportunities for positive impact.' Comalapa is a cushion handwoven by women artisans in Guatemala. It is made from rapidly renewable, locally grown, undyed cotton. The simultaneously bold yet subtle relief graphic is intended as a sampler of various traditional patterns found in Mayan culture.

Buoy Brushes
Green & Associates

Coffee grounds, eggshells, pig bristles

www.ganda.org
ooobject.com

Green & Associates is a group of designers based in Beijing who design and produce objects for the home made from a wide range of unusual organic compounds. Making use of some well-known recyclable materials available in vast quantities, such as eggshells and coffee grounds, they have created unusual biodegradable compounds for use in the production of brushes.

With over 501 billion cups consumed every year, coffee is one of the world's most popular drinks. This leads to a huge amount of waste coffee grounds that can be used to constitute new material. The handle of the Buoy Coffee Brush is made up of 35 per cent coffee grounds collected from local restaurants.

Likewise, the Buoy Egg Brush contains 35 per cent discarded eggshell collected from farms in Beijing. With over 45 million tonnes of eggs produced in China in 2006, this is clearly a material in plentiful supply.

Citrus Juicer
Green & Associates

Bio-plastic

www.ganda.org
ooobject.com

Chinese design studio Green & Associates use well-known recyclable organic materials to make their products. While some of these may contain ingredients such as peanut shells or sweet potato, their Citrus Juicer is rather aptly made of a material derived partly from orange peel.

The earliest known example of juicer, dating back to the eighteenth century and found in Turkey, was made of clay. While this design from modern China is perhaps no more sustainable than that one, it certainly makes a statement about the possibilities of imaginative and experimental design.

BlockHanger
Green Furniture Sweden

Mixed woods
D: 7.5 cm (3 in), Diam.: 5.5 cm (2⅛ in)

greenfurniture.se

BlockHanger is a robust wall knob made from leftover mixed woods from Green Furniture's own carpenter in Lammhult, Sweden. Sold in a pack of four pieces, the simple design and unique composition of the individual hangers is intended to allow the creation of a wall that is 'joyfully functional'. A screw comes included with the knob; after mounting the knob on the wall, the screw is hidden with a small round of naturally tanned Swedish leather.

For every box sold, Green Furniture plant a birch tree for use in the production of future furniture.

Black Beauties
Ineke Hans

Recycled plastic
Various sizes

www.inekehans.com

Black Beauties is a growing collection of products for children by Dutch designer Ineke Hans. Each object is made from black recycled plastic, partly for the simple reason that the raw material is readily available in black, but also to give the impression of a 3D pictogram. Being made entirely from solid plastic, the designs are suitable for indoor and outdoor play, or even in the bath.

While many products for children are bright and garish, the Black Beauties aim to show that children do not only react to colours, but very often they respond to shapes, opportunities and new ways of playing with things.

Soundwave Geo
Ineke Hans for Offecct

Recycled PET
H: 58.5 cm (23 in), W: 58.5 cm (23 in), D: 6 cm (2⅜ in)

www.inekehans.com
www.offecct.se

Swedish manufacturer Offecct create products for noisy workplaces, like this sound-absorbing acoustic panel. The Soundwave Geo is made entirely from recycled PET plastics, but has a tactile, fuzzy surface similar to felt. Although made for a practical purpose, the panel has a geometric design in relief, courtesy of Dutch furniture designer Ineke Hans, making it a decorative as well as functional object.

Responding to an increase in office noise pollution, the panels help reduce disturbing reflections of background sounds such as voices, telephones and traffic to provide a more tranquil working environment.

The Devar
Hendzel + Hunt

Scrap wood
H: 32 cm (12⅝ in), W: 20 cm (7⅞ in)

www.hendzelandhunt.com

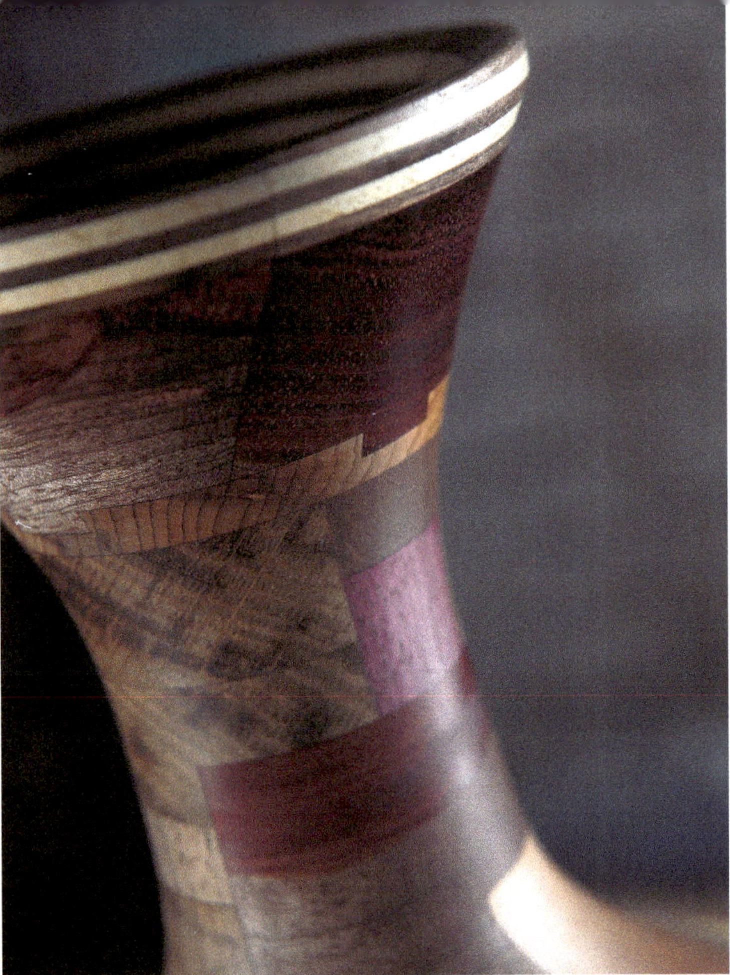

Hendzel + Hunt are furniture designers and makers who use their local area as an open resource, gathering waste materials from the streets of South London and transforming them into bespoke items such as the Devar vase. Although highly finished, the patchwork nature of the vase makes no attempt to hide its origins, telling the story of miscellaneous scrap woods, much of which came from discarded pallets.

In this way the company aim to create objects that exude intrigue and character, alongside a high level of craftsmanship, showcasing what can be achieved within small batch production.

For more on Hendzel + Hunt, see the Q&A on page 224.

Matka Vase
Pepe Heykoop

Recycled stainless steel, scrap leather
H: 28 cm (11 in), W: 26 cm (10¼ in)

www.pepeheykoop.nl

Matka Vases are designed by Pepe Heykoop and produced in his workshop located in one of the poorest neighborhoods in Mumbai, India, providing meaningful jobs, income and hope for its neediest residents (see pages 148–49).

The vases were designed using recycled matkas (traditional Indian stainless steel water carriers) and scrap leather. The concept is partly a reaction to the huge amount of high-quality leather wasted by the furniture industry, which can be up to 30 per cent.

Each vase contains a unique and personal story, both of its previous owner and the person who gave it new life and use.

Q&A: Hendzel + Hunt

Jan Hendzel and Oscar Hunt met whilst working for a cabinetmaker, and started their own studio, Hendzel + Hunt, six years ago. Their Made in Peckham range of high-end furniture, created entirely from reclaimed and waste materials, debuted at London Design Week 2010 and launched them onto the design scene.

www.hendzelandhunt.com

Hendzel + Hunt's Gowlett stools are constructed from discarded wooden pallets.

How would you describe your style?
Process is an integral part of our work – the material sets
a direction and drives the narrative, to which we add our
understanding of joinery in an effort to bring all the parts
together in an interesting way. We strive to give as much
consideration to the obvious details as to the hidden
parts, often overlooked. We try to excel technically, and
see every project as an opportunity to innovate our
approach in a manner that showcases the beauty of
reclaimed materials.

In what way is your work sustainable?
The original Made in Peckham range was produced
entirely with waste and reclaimed material from one
postal-code area. Sourcing materials from our doorstep
not only reduces the carbon footprint but also creates a
relationship with the area that is unique to our practice.
We do our best to seek the provenance of our materials
and incorporate their former use into the product, which
helps give each project a unique identity. We have
created many of our iconic pieces from timbers sourced
in Peckham, and although we have a mix of local and
international clients, we are always trying to attain an
honest level of sustainable practice.

What materials and techniques do you use?
Timber is the most abundant resource for us. Using
handcrafted techniques alongside the potential of digital
machining, and juxtaposing conventional and Japanese
joinery methods, combined with complex geometry,
exemplifies our methods of adapting traditional concepts
of furniture making to fit the demands of our projects.

**What are you working on at the moment, and what
do you hope to work on in the future?**
Currently, we are working on numerous projects for
private and commercial clients. We have been actively
seeking exciting commissions and competitions that
allow us to excel as a studio. We are doing our first large-
scale project in the public realm. It's very exciting, poetic
and a scale up from what we are used to.

As for the future we want to develop the Made in
Peckham range, refining it to reflect the expertise we
now hold in working with reclaimed timbers, as well as
create a whole new range of furniture. We will also be
pushing our 24hr design challenge series, which is an
experimental platform for designer makers based on
the ideas of Made in Peckham. We hope to bring it to
an international audience and create a global cross-
pollination of varied crafts skills.

**Have you noticed any particular trends
in sustainable design?**
When we started out, there were a lot of people using
reclaimed materials to create products, which we found
to be lacking in originality. The trend for reusing materials
was not highly associated with craftsmanship, and
only a few pieces stood out from the DIY aesthetic of
reassembling pieces of wood. Now it seems the overall
quality of reclaimed furniture is much better. Consumers
are more aware of quality and interested in the process
of making and good craftsmanship. A growing sense
of awareness within sustainable design has impacted
on designers in terms of what they are making and on
consumers in terms of what and why they are buying.

**What materials or techniques do you think we'll be
seeing more of in the future?**
We believe the general awareness of sustainable
principles will become even more embedded in the
design process, which will lead designers to structure
their work around what is available. Nonetheless, the
quick evolution of 3D printing will have an impact on the
materials that will be used and will also radically change
the ideas around maker vs consumer, alternating roles
and allowing people to design what they need. But the
true craftsman will still work in the best tradition whilst
using digital technology when necessary.

Gemma Box
Gemma Holt for Discipline

Ash, walnut or oak
L: 13 cm (5⅛ in), W: 7.5 cm (3 in), H: 5 cm (2 in)
L: 18.5 cm (7¼ in), W: 9 cm (3½ in), H: 7 cm (2¾ in)
L: 13 cm (5⅛ in), W: 5 cm (2 in), H: 7.5 cm (3 in)
L: 18.5 cm (7¼ in), W: 7 cm (2¾ in), H: 9 cm (3½ in)

gemmaholt.co.uk
www.discipline.eu

Relying on the noble beauty of wood, these minimalist boxes by London-based artist and designer Gemma Holt look like nothing more than oblong blocks of sustainable oak, ash or walnut. However, the top side is in fact a snugly fitting lid, held in place by invisible magnets, allowing the box to be used for storing secret items.

This efficient use of sustainable materials makes for a very pleasing piece.

OS WaterBoiler
Jesse Howard & Thomas Lomée for OpenStructures

Various housing, plumbing and electrical components
Various sizes

intrastructures.net
openstructures.net

WaterBoiler is an appliance that uses OS (OpenStructures) design principles to explore an adaptable and scalable production process. The OS world is designed according to the Wikipedia model, where supporters contribute towards a common pool of modular parts, components and structures, rather than designing in isolation. Intended as a form of collaborative Meccano to which the broadest range of people from craftsmen to multinationals can participate, the project envisions 'a new standard for sustainable design that facilitates the reuse of parts and components and allows us to build things together'.

With its transparent construction, and design capable of complete disassembly, the WaterBoiler invites users to adapt, repair and combine with existing OS components.

Paper Pencils
Ruben Iglesias
for Droog

Magazines, catalogues, graphite
L: 17 cm (6¾ in), Diam.: 0.6 cm (¼ in)

www.droog.com

Created by Ruben Iglesias for Droog, Paper Pencils use recycled material from discarded local newspapers and magazines in place of wood, by simply rolling paper around the graphite core, using as little glue as possible. In addition to saving trees, each of these unique pencils is handmade in the Netherlands as part of a charity project.

The pencils are part of a broader enterprise called UP. This is an investigative economic model that aims to increase the value of dead stock through redesign. An alternative to recycling and disposal, UP treats leftover goods as raw material for creative reinterpretation in order to bring leftovers back into circulation.

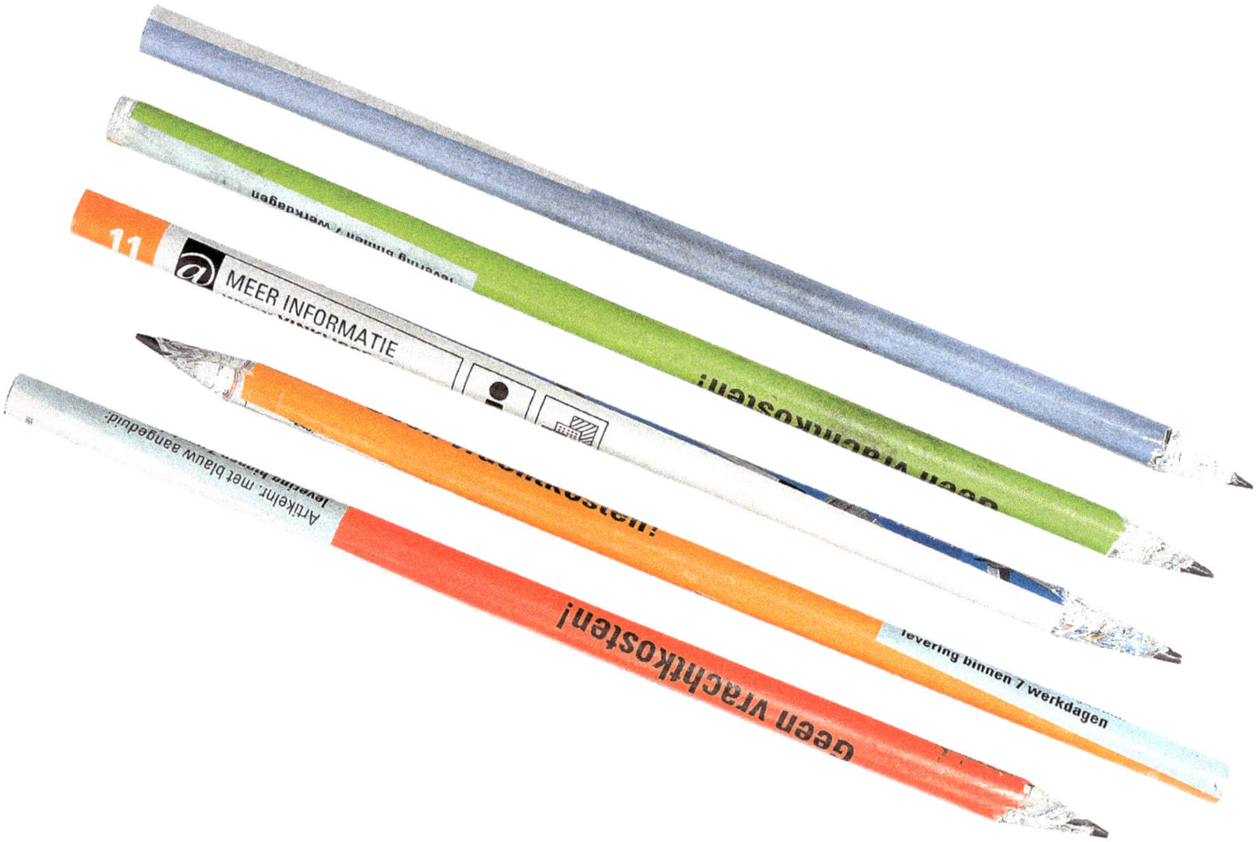

Animal Print Rug
Cordula Kehrer with Editions in Craft

Straw

www.cordulakehrer.de
www.editionsincraft.com

A natural and sustainable material employed since the dawn of agricultural societies, straw has traditionally been used to construct everything from roofs to baskets, carpets and ceremonial objects. Today, the material is often considered old-fashioned, and straw work is currently one of the most challenged crafts in the Nordic region. Due to the low cost of labour and handwork in foreign countries, what was once a ommonly performed skill by women in the Swedish city of Dalsland, in particular, is now rapidly disappearing.

Woven from straw, this rug by German designer Cordula Kehrer was created at Farmer's Gold, a workshop organized by Editions in Craft (see also page 51). Held in 2012 in Dalsland, the workshop allowed participants to exchange ideas and techniques, combine local tradition with modern practice, and explore the possibilities of straw and craft in a contemporary market.

While this rug may be fun, there are serious ecological advantages to straw as a raw material – it grows locally, is available in abundance, is extremely cheap and is suited to a wide range of applications.

Wooden Vessels
Eleanor Lakelin

Oak, ash, chestnut, holly
Various sizes

eleanorlakelin.co.uk

Eleanor Lakelin's work celebrates natural forms and textures in the form of contemporary wooden bowls, vessels and sculpture. Employing traditional turning and carving techniques with lathes and chisels, Lakelin uses only sustainably felled wood from British trees, often from within a 3-mile radius of her London workshop. Wherever possible, the products are supplied with the details of their origins.

She is particularly drawn to the beauty in decay, and to the rich and unusual effects of the passage of time, fungus and insects on different woods, much of which would otherwise be thrown away for its irregularities.

Amaurodes
Lanzavecchia + Wai
for Nodus

Wool, bamboo silk
Diam.: 220 cm (86½ in)

lanzavecchia-wai.com
www.nodusrug.it

Amaurodes is a hand-tufted rug, woven from wool and bamboo silk by Italian manufacturer Nodus. Bamboo silk is an organic product from sustainable bamboo sources, and the rug is ethically certified by GoodWeave International.

Lanzavecchia + Wai's motif of a fictitious insect called *Amaurodes chernobilis* is a warning about the effects of nuclear radiation on living beings, and the very real ramifications of events such as the Chernobyl disaster for biology and ecology. The mutated insect is intended to illustrate the effects of mankind's activities, many of which create unknown ripples into the future, and highlight the fragility of our planet.

Pupazzi
La Quercia 21
(Luca De Pascalis &
Nicola Gubiotti)

Reclaimed wood, textiles, metal
Various sizes

www.laquercia21.it

La Quercia 21's Pupazzi, or 'Puppets', are a family of about 30 lacquered box-containers made from reclaimed materials and found objects that would otherwise be thrown away. They form a set of playful and spontaneous designs.

Although the makers follow a rough template, the Pupazzi are all unique, ranging from vintage furniture and retro appliances to old scrapped robots and vaguely zoomorphic figures. The exact form of each puppet is dictated by whatever raw materials are available to hand at the time, such as wood offcuts, scraps of fabric and rusted ironmongery. They are then finished off in pastel colours and coated in natural lacquer.

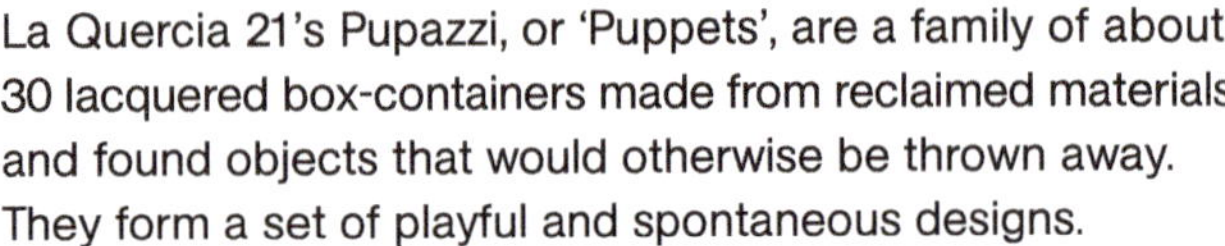

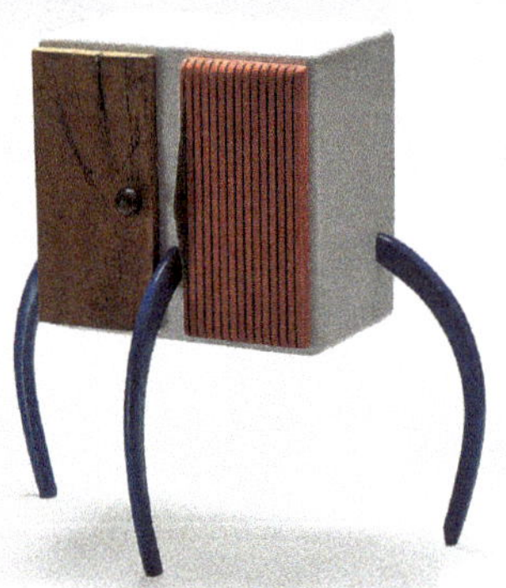

Paperwork
Hannah Lobley

Paper
Various sizes

www.hl-web.net

After accidently leaving a book out in the rain, Hannah Lobley developed Paperwork, a recycling technique where printed pages from unwanted books and papers are layered and transformed back into a solid wood-like material. Paperwork allows the manufacture of tactile, adaptable products and is well suited to recycling obsolete material like telephone directories.

The finished material is shaped using traditional woodworking methods, and the patterns created in the worked material even resemble the natural grain of wood. This leads to unique surface decoration and allows simple geometric designs to take on a new level of interest.

Arbor House
Loll Designs

Arbor Wood, recycled HDPE
H: 18 cm (7⅛ in), W: 17 cm (6¾ in), D: 20 cm (7⅞ in)

www.lolldesigns.com
arborwoodco.com

American manufacturer Loll Designs' Arbor House is an eco-friendly home for birds made from Arbor Wood and 100 per cent recycled and recyclable high-density polyethylene (HDPE).

Arbor Wood is a durable, all-weather wood created from locally harvested maple. The process uses heat and steam to modify the cell structure of wood, making it highly resistant to rot, as well as expansion and contraction, without the use of chemicals. By using varying cook temperatures, a range of colour options within a single species can be achieved without the use of stains. A tree is then planted for each order received.

Loll Designs run their production schedule with a delay to allow orders of similar colours to build up and thus cut more parts at one time to utilize more of the raw material. The products are then flat-packed in 100 per cent post-consumer recycled packaging.

Loowatt
Loowatt

Various materials
Various sizes

www.loowatt.com

Loowatt is a waterless toilet system that seals human waste into biodegradable polymer film for anaerobic digestion (AD). AD converts the waste and film into bio-gas, which can be used directly as fuel or converted to electricity, and digestate, a nutrient-rich liquid that is further treated and sold as fertilizer.

Traditional inorganic fertilizers are produced using huge amounts of non-renewable energy and are valued according to markets linked to oil prices. By using locally produced digestate, poorer countries are able to avoid this expense and ensure more reliable food production. In addition, by providing a source of combustible energy, the system lessens demand for fossil fuels or locally gathered wood, easing deforestation and associated problems such as desertification.

Loowatt's most obvious quality of being waterless has secondary benefits too. Apart from saving enormous amounts of precious water in developing countries, the system avoids polluting run-off into watercourses, helping to prevent the spread of disease.

Papyrus Storage Boxes
Madwa

Papyrus reeds
Various sizes

www.madwa.com

These boldly patterned storage boxes are woven from sustainable papyrus reeds by artisans in northern Madagascar. The weavers work in collaboration with Madwa, a 'social upliftment' project employing artisans in Madagascar, Mozambique, Swaziland and South Africa.

Madwa believes that trade is the most effective and sustainable way for individuals to lift themselves out of poverty, and is committed to empowering people to use their craft skills to achieve economic stability and independence. The enterprise also keeps local traditions alive by encouraging young people to learn declining skills.

Foodscapes
Michela Milani
with Whomade

Peanut husks, carrot peel, potato starch
Various sizes

www.michelamilani.com
www.whomade.it

Foodscapes is a collection of seed-shaped, textured tableware created from food waste. Made from peanut husks or carrot peel, then mixed with potato starch, the designs are moulded from a mash of edible leftovers, free of additives, colorants, thickeners or any other artificial agents. This means they are perfectly suited to being composted when they are no longer needed, where they will make healthy fertilizer for growing new food.

Textiles by Mumo
Mumo

Fairtrade organic cotton
Up to L: 90 cm (35⅜ in), W: 90 cm (35⅜ in)

www.mumo-uk.com

This UK-based company works with ethically produced fabrics to make bold and colourful homewares, inspired by the local art and culture of the regions where these fabrics are made. Collections so far have been inspired by Rio de Janeiro's urban-beach lifestyle and the 'Tropicalia' movement that defined Brazilian art and music in the late 60s and 70s.

One of modern Brazil's main problems is centralization of wealth in huge urban centres, causing large-scale migration from rural areas to the cities, and resulting in shanty towns (favelas), where living conditions are basic, often dangerous and catch people in a cycle of poverty.

Sourcing cotton from Paraiba, northeastern Brazil, Mumo pays around double the market price to a local cooperative of over 300 farmers, providing an important source of income where poverty levels are high. Mumo also pays for the organic certification process so that they can trade in similar ways with other companies and increase their income in a sustainable way.

In addition, one of Mumo's manufacturers in the UK is the back-to-work programme Textiles By St Anne's, a group of highly skilled seamstresses who have had problems with mental illness.

Bicicleta
Nanimarquina
(Nani Marquina & Ariadna Miquel)

100% recycled rubber
L: 240 cm (94½ in), W: 170 cm (66⅞ in)

www.nanimarquina.com

Contemplating the enormous volume of bicycle traffic on a trip to India, designer Nani Marquina realized that the huge number of worn-out inner tubes this generated could provide a useful resource.

The result was Bicicleta, a new carpet collection that pays homage to the country's most popular mode of transport, made entirely from this recycled rubber. Raising awareness of recycled products, each of these conceptual, yet practical, rugs is made using between 130 and 140 bicycle inner tubes, all collected, processed and woven by hand in India.

Kala
Nanimarquina
with Care & Fair

New Zealand wool
Thickness: 2 cm (5 in)

www.nanimarquina.com
www.care-fair.org

The Kala project is the result of a partnership between design company Nanimarquina and Care & Fair, an initiative that works against illegal child labour and supports workers in the rug-making industry in India, Pakistan and Nepal.

In Hindi, *kala* means 'tomorrow' as well as 'art', an apt title for a collection created using original drawings from students at Care & Fair schools in India. Supporting children's creativity and imagination is the organization's strategy for helping them secure a better future.

For each rug sold, 150 euros goes to help fund the new Care & Fair school in Bhadohi, India.

Bottleware
Nendo for Coca-Cola

Recycled glass
Various sizes

www.nendo.jp

The Nendo Bottleware collection is a series of five
dishes and bowls in simple shapes that enhance the
fine air bubbles and distortions that are a hallmark
of recycled glass.

Produced by glassblowers in the Aomori prefecture of
Japan, the collection is made from Coca-Cola bottles that
have deteriorated over the course of extensive recycling,
and can no longer be used for their original purpose.
To capture the spirit of the iconic bottle in the new
products, Nendo opted to retain its distinctive lower
shape, as though the top had been sliced off, in addition
to its particular green tint – known as 'Georgia Green'.

Bear Rug
Node (Nadia Shireen)

Tibetan wool, natural dyes
L: 183 cm (72 in), W: 120 cm (47¼ in)

www.madebynode.com

Part of the Node rug collection, Nadia Shireen's Bear Rug is made from pure Tibetan wool and produced entirely by hand using traditional Tibetan carpet-making techniques. The wool is hand-spun into thread, then hand-dyed with natural and non-polluting dyes.

Node is a non-profit social business, which aims to combine design with fairtrade manufacturing. The project is run in collaboration with the Kumbeshwar Technical School in Kathmandu, set up by the Khadgi family, who are from the lowest caste in Nepal. Having used waste from their work as cleaners to establish a successful fertilizer business, the Khadgis have now set up a weaving school, using their wealth to help the rest of their caste out of poverty.

As well as being given fair wages, their weavers are taught literacy and skills. In addition to training adults with profits from the sales of the rugs, the Khadgis also provide a school of 260 pupils with free books and meals, and fund an orphanage for 25 children.

No bears are harmed in the making of this rug.

For more on Node, see the Q&A on page 244.

Denim Denim Rug
Nudie Jeans

Denim
L: 200cm (78¾ in), W: 150 cm (59 in)

www.nudiejeans.com

This recycled rag rug from Swedish label Nudie Jeans gives new life to worn-out jeans and scraps of waste denim, and has been labelled an example of 'Good Environmental Re-design' by the Swedish Society for Nature Conservation.

As part of the brand's 'Post-recycled Jeans' initiative, these Scandinavian-style rugs are produced in Turkey in collaboration with Nudie's organic denim supplier, Bossa. Remnants of old jeans are cut down to serrated strips that are then sewn together and rolled up on spools. The strips are then woven together by hand on a manual shuttle loom in an exacting and time-consuming process. The weft is made from indigo-dyed thread, the same that is used in a pair of Nudie Jeans.

There is probably no rug that can withstand heavy use as well as a rag rug, and being made from high-quality, tough denim, this rug can be expected to last a very long time.

Q&A: Node

Chris Haughton and Akshay Sthapit set up Node to connect international buyers and designers with local weavers in Nepal. Node is a nonprofit, socially responsible company, and sales of rugs support a school and orphanage in Nepal. Their project has gathered momentum, and they exhibited 18 rugs in the Design Museum in London in 2013.

madebynode.com

Node connects a worldwide network of designers and artists with traditional Nepalese carpet makers to create beautiful handmade rugs.

In what way are Node's products sustainable?
All the rugs are made using the traditional techniques
from Tibet. The wool is unbleached and uses non-toxic
dyes. Tibetan wool is famous for its durability; the sheep
are bred for their tough, weather-resistant wool, so rugs
made from it will be around for generations. We had
also woven rugs from banana fibres, which is a waste
material in Nepal, but it's just not as hard-wearing as the
wool. Although we try to be as sustainable as we can,
our main objective was to set ourselves up as a social
business, to help grow the weaving cooperative and
help people.

Kumbeshwar, the workshop we work with, has an
amazing story. It was set up in the 80s by the Khadgi
family, who are from what would traditionally be seen
as a low caste. To help the rest of his caste out of
poverty, the grandfather set up an adult training centre
to teach literacy, weaving and carpentry – all this from
his home! The workshop has now expanded and has
trained six thousand adults and funded a school of 250
and an orphanage of 25. I think education and getting
people into a stable position so that they are able to
plan for their future is crucial for a sustainable future.
Sustainability is not an option for the very poor, which
is why the poorest countries are often the ones with the
worst environmental damage.

Which artists do you work with?
For the Design Museum collection, in order to make
an interesting collection, we approached 18 artists for
their diversity within design. We have graphic designers,
illustrators, fashion designers, textile designers and
picture-book authors, but all were chosen for their
graphic suitability for designing rugs. Although we
approached some of the top names in their fields for no
fee, no one we approached turned down this project.

Donna Wilson was awarded Elle Decoration British
Designer of the Year 2011. USA-based artist Geoff
McFetridge is one of the best-known illustrators working
today; he was art director of the Beastie Boys' magazine
Grand Royal and featured in the film *Beautiful Losers*.
Canadian Jon Klassen is the illustrator/author of the best-
selling children's book *This Is Not My Hat*. Sanna Annukka
is a Finnish illustrator and textile artist well known for her
prints and patterns for Marimekko.

What materials and techniques do you use?
Wool, yarn and dye – and nothing else!
machining, and juxtaposing conventional and Japanese

What are your plans for the future?
More exhibitions, but nothing confirmed just yet.
We are weaving a rug with Oliver Jeffers for his exhibition
next month. We have several custom rugs weaving for
different designers, and even a restaurant in London.
We offer a service for anyone to design their own rug,
which is proving very popular. We just want to encourage
more exciting designers to get involved in fair trade, that's
our objective.

Rug makers in Node's workshop,
Kumbeshwar, are paid fair wages
and taught literacy and skills.

In addition, their work supports a
school and an orphanage.

Banbury Rugs
Roger Oates

British wool
Various sizes

www.rogeroates.com

Roger Oates's upcycled rugs are woven from hundreds of spools of good-quality dyed wool no longer required by the carpet industry and earmarked for disposal.

The company aspired to create a collection of rugs that would not only make use of the wool but be beautiful in their own right as well. The rugs are a return to the company's roots, initially making rag rugs from old cloth. Oates champions upcycling over recycling, as it does not require the energy and resources of industrial collecting, sorting and processing.

Fire Hose Mats
Oxgut Hose Co.

Firehoses, polypropylene
L: 91 cm (35⅞ in), W: 60cm (23⅝ in)
L: 152 cm (59⅞ in), W: 60cm (23⅝ in)
L: 122 cm (48 in), W: 91 cm (35⅞ in)

oxgut.com
childburn.org

Oxgut's recycled mats are handmade in California using recycled fire hose salvaged from US fire departments. Named in honour of the very first fire-fighting hoses in ancient Greece, the company rescues literally tonnes of hoses each year, discarded once they are no longer in top-class fire-fighting condition (see also page 89).

However, the designers at Oxgut have found them to be perfectly suited to a number of applications, such as their Fire Hose Mats, which piece together strips of contrasting colours and textures.

As well as avoiding tonnes of wasteful landfill, Oxgut donate a portion of their annual proceeds to the Children's Burn Foundation.

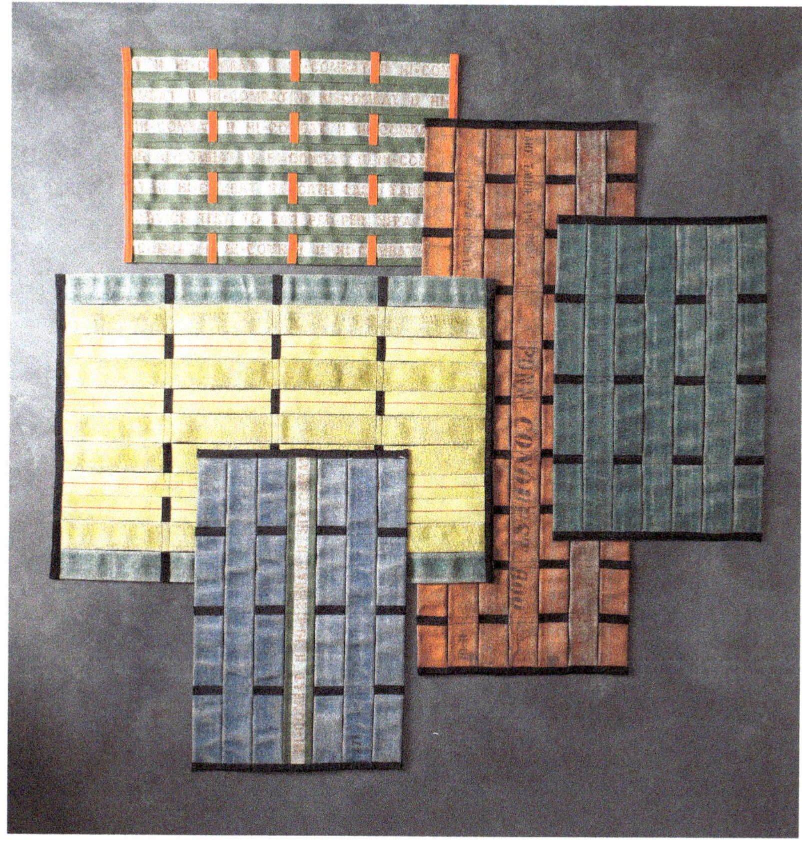

No.1 Cotton Dhurrie Collection

Oyyo

Organic cotton, vegetable dyes
Various sizes

oyyo.se

Dhurries are thick, flat-woven rugs, traditionally used in India as floor coverings or meditation mats. The Oyyo No.1 Cotton Dhurrie collection consists of a series of six original dhurries, handwoven by a community of craftspeople near India's 'Blue City', Jodhpur.

The dhurries are woven without machines, using centuries-old techniques, but with contemporary designs and palettes. Their vivid colours and bold patterns are intended as a statement of Oyyo's optimism and core values, claiming a re-engagement with the natural world and expressing confidence in the productive wonders made possible by cultural diversity.

Each rug is made from 100 per cent organic cotton and coloured with vegetable dyes derived from local plants. In addition, dyes are fixed with soda ash, iron vinegar and aluminium salts, rather than harmful traditional mordants such as heavy-metal-rich alum.

Akasma
Satyendra Pakhalé
with RSVP

Recycled, reused coloured flat glass
Various sizes

www.satyendra-pakhale.com

Akasma is a small collection of baskets and trays made by RSVP in conjunction with Satyendra Pakhalé. RSVP is a small Italian manufacturer of everyday glass products, created from leftover remnants of industrial bent glass from larger architectural applications.

Each of the Akasma designs comprise two identical profiles, cut from a flat glass sheet, then bent and glued on to a round glass base. Each of these steps was an extreme technical challenge, requiring precision cutting and accurate bending to fit the pieces to the base while aligning with each other along their edges.

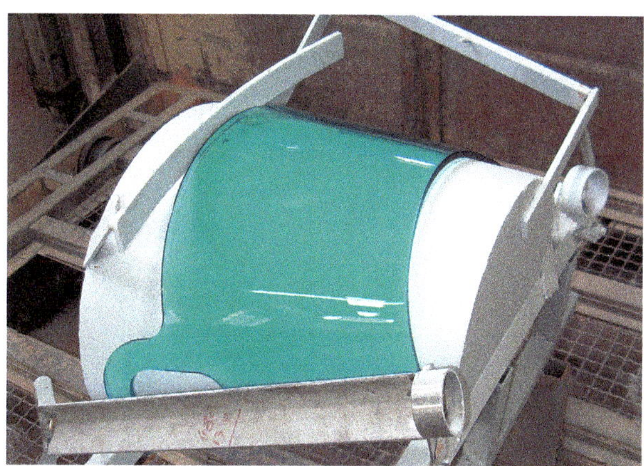

Blantyre Jar
People of the Sun

Recycled glass, wood
Various sizes

www.peopleofthesun.net

Blantyre jars are handmade from local materials by artisans in the southern region of Malawi. The jar itself is made from a recycled wine bottle, cut by hand using a clever trick with rope, fire and cold water. It is then sanded with three different stones in degrees of roughness to achieve the desired smoothness.
The distinctive lids are made from local mahogany hardwood, shaped by hand on a lathe.

People of the Sun aspire to create opportunities for low-income artisans in Malawi, combining indigenous knowledge with contemporary design and innovation and reinvesting profits into their social mission (see also pages 85, 108).

Patchwork Cushions
Place de Bleu

Waste fabric
Various sizes

www.placedebleu.dk

Place de Bleu is a non-profit home interiors and accessories company, which provides employment for immigrant women in Denmark. The company assists women who have so far failed to find a foothold in the Danish labour market – often because of language difficulties or illness – helping them to make the most of their exceptional skills while also helping to preserve ancient handcraft techniques that have been inherited through many generations of women from all over the world.

All the pieces are limited edition and made by hand, sewn, crocheted or embroidered in Place de Bleu's workshop in Copenhagen. The products are made using surplus materials from the Danish textile manufacturer Kvadrat, thus ensuring both high product quality and sustainability of production.

Textiles
Catarina Riccabona

Wool, linen, hemp
Various sizes

catarinariccabona.com

Weaver Catarina Riccabona's range of sustainable textiles is created from a broad selection of eco-friendly resources. For the warp threads in her throws and cushions, she uses undyed recycled linen, avoiding intensive industrial bleaching and colouring processes, and the enormous amounts of water that accompany them. The linen is from a British company that specializes in re-spinning yarn that is considered industrial waste, such as surplus from carpet factories.

For the weft yarn, Riccabona often uses second-hand material received through donations. She also makes use of undyed alpaca wool from the UK, chosen for its exceptional deep black, warm chocolate brown and creamy white natural colours.

In the event of needing a specific, unusual colour, Riccabona employs a specialist supplier from Finland who dyes local Finnsheep wool to order with mushrooms, bark and botanical dyes from her garden.

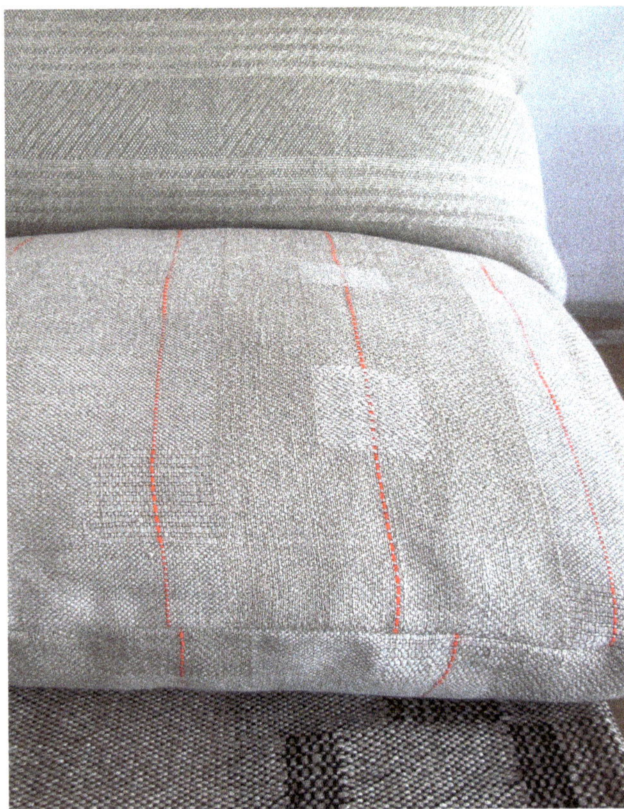

Rush Bowls
RushMatters
(Felicity Irons)

Freshwater bulrush, jute twine
Various sizes

www.rushmatters.co.uk

These rush bowls by Felicity Irons of RushMatters are woven from English freshwater bulrushes using traditional techniques going back many centuries.

With a few select helpers, Irons harvests the rushes in the summer months from a number of local rivers. The rush is cut from punts using rush knifes, a slim scythe-shaped blade 1m (3ft) long, fixed to a 2m (6ft) handle, enabling stems to be cut from deep down on the river bed. The rush beds grow back fully within two years.

Up to 2 tonnes of rush is cut each day, transported back to the farm and stood against a hedge to dry in the sun and wind. The variation in weather during this process naturally produces extraordinary and beautiful shades of colour. Prolonged sun gently bleaches to warm honey tones, while windy weather lends the colours a more vivid green/blue hue.

Rush Matting
RushMatters
(Felicity Irons)

Freshwater bulrush
Various sizes

www.rushmatters.co.uk

Based at Grange Farm in Bedfordshire, England, Felicity Irons's company produces a wide range of woven rush products, from baskets and bags to hats and furniture (see page 253). The core of their work, though, is traditional rush floor matting, also known as medieval or apple matting.

The rush is plaited by hand and interwoven with lavender, artemesia and camomile into 10 cm (3⅞ in)-wide lengths, and hand-sewn together with jute twine. Each mat is made to the client's requirements as a central mat or runner, or fitted as a carpet, wall to wall. Once laid, the matting benefits from regular watering using an atomizer. This rejuvenates the rush work and enhances the aroma and overall life of the flooring.

From cutting and gathering to drying and weaving, the whole process is entirely natural, with no chemicals used at any stage.

Trecia
Salamanca Design
(Lucy Salamanca)

Agave fibre
Various sizes

www.salamancadesign.com

Trecia rugs are handmade in Colombia from fibres of the agave plant, using traditional local weaving techniques.

Conceived by Italian-Colombian designer Lucy Salamanca, the rugs form part of the broader Amate collection, made in three different Latin American countries by four different groups of craftspeople, each chosen to meet ethical and sustainability criteria. All fibres and other raw materials used are recycled and/or from natural sources, and all the processes are exclusively carried out by hand, from the harvest to the final product.

The Amate collection aims to create a network of individual producers, techniques and materials, enabling manufacturers to pool their experiences and production techniques in order to broaden their horizons.

Rope Mats
Serpent Sea
(Sophie Aschauer)

Rope
Various sizes

www.serpentsea.com

Sophie Aschauer was inspired to make woven mats out of discarded marine rope after a sailing trip to Nantucket Island. Rope is often used in critical and potentially dangerous situations and has to be in excellent condition, otherwise it should be replaced. This leads to a lot of rope being thrown away that is perfectly suited to less demanding applications. Since the rope is designed for use in harsh ocean environments, these mats are ideal for use both indoors and out.

Aschauer's rope comes from different sources, such as a boatyard in Connecticut, a rope factory, and climbing rope discarded after heavy falls. She has never had to buy any new material and works exclusively with rope that would otherwise be thrown away.

Each mat is unique and woven by hand using one of four different knots – Aschauer refers to as Bonny, Drake, Morgan and Killigrew, after the notorious seventeenth-century pirates. Each of these knots has a long tradition, having been tied for centuries by sailors for practical purposes as well as for ornamentation.

Coiled Vases
Siyazama Project & BCXSY
for Editions in Craft

Beads, plastic fabric
H: 20 cm (7⅞ in), Diam.: 12 cm (4¾ in)
H: 27 cm (10⅝ in), Diam.: 16 cm (6¼ in)
H: 30 cm (11¾ in), Diam.: 24 cm (9½ in)

www.siyazamaproject.dut.ac.za
www.editionsincraft.com

Coiled Vases are produced in a collaboration between BCXSY and the Siyazama Project, a collective of 20 women from the rural province of KwaZulu-Natal in South Africa who specialize in traditional beadwork (see also page 258).

In researching the beadwork of Siyazama, BCXSY found their inspiration in traditional ceramics, constructed from handmade coils of clay. Associated with the natural movements of a snake, they wanted the beadwork to be suggestive of the scales on a snakeskin, both in pattern and colour.

Each vase features different shapes and designs. They are made from locally found and recycled materials in order to keep the production process simple. The bases are made from recycled plastic bottles and discarded pieces of fabric, covered with strands of beads.

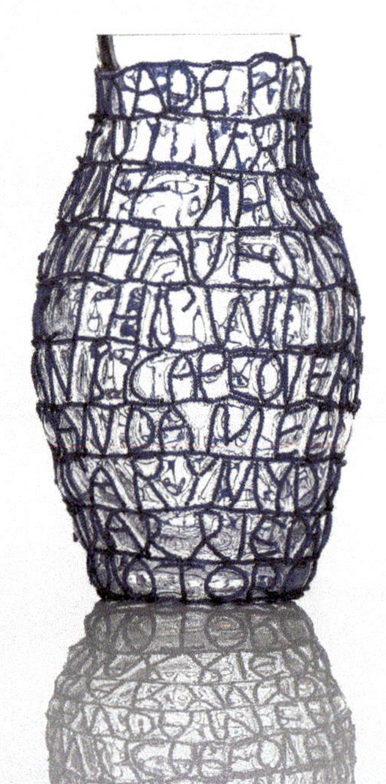

Story Vases
Sizayama Project & Front
for Editions in Craft

Beads, wire, glass
Various sizes

www.siyazamaproject.dut.ac.za
www.frontdesign.se
www.editionsincraft.com

Story Vases is a project initiated by Swedish designers Front to create a series of vases that tell the stories of five members of the Sizayama Project, living in remote villages in KwaZulu-Natal, South Africa (see page 257).

The designs record the testimonies of each woman in glass beads threaded on to wire – a traditional Zulu craft technique that provides work for many women in South Africa. The beaded wires are constructed around vase-shaped moulds, in which glass is then blown by Swedish master glassblower Reino Björk.

With these vases, Front used its conceptual approach to design, material and narrative to explore new ways of working with Zulu bead craft in collaboration with local artisans. This long-term project aims to broaden the market for the craft, and to let these women's stories be heard by more people.

Autarchy
Studio Formafantasma

Flour, agricultural waste, limestone
Various sizes

www.formafantasma.com

Autarchy is a conceptual installation, displaying a hypothetical scenario of a community embracing a serene and self-inflicted embargo where nature is cultivated, harvested and processed, to feed and make tools to serve human needs. In the installation, a collection of functional and durable vessels and lamps, naturally desiccated or low-temperature baked, are produced with a bio-material composed of 70 per cent flour, 20 per cent agricultural waste and 10 per cent natural limestone.

The differences in the colour palette are obtained by the selection of distinct vegetables, spices and roots that are dried, boiled or filtered for their natural dyes. *Autarchy* suggests an alternative way of producing goods where inherited knowledge is used to find sustainable and uncomplicated solutions.

Cork
Studio Noam Dover
(Michal Cederbaum)

Raw cork
Various sizes

www.noamdover.com
www.19greekstreet.com

This collection of cork bowls is the outcome of a collaboration between Michal Cederbaum of Israel's Studio Noam Dover and OpusDV, a furniture company based in Portugal and Israel.

Relying on the pure, tactile appeal of raw cork, with all its flaws and imperfections, the unrefined nature of the finished bowls is typical of Studio Noam Dover's aspirations to 'create objects that reveal both their essence and the process of making'.

One of cork's important sustainability factors rests on its CO_2-absorbing potential. Trees that have their bark stripped every nine years for industrial applications absorb three to five times as much CO_2 than similar trees that are left idle. Through this serendipitous process, the cork industry goes some way to offsetting its own emissions.

tado°

tado°

www.tado.com

An intelligent, digital management system for domestic heating supplies, tado° can be controlled via a smartphone. By using geolocation technology and tracking the user's comings and goings, it allows the most efficient possible use of fuel.

Based on the premise that a third of the energy consumed around the world is used for heating or cooling buildings, tado° aims to minimize energy wastage by replacing outdated, non-smart technology.

Essentially the system ensures that the user's home is not being heated while it is empty, but that it is always warm on their return. In addition, it checks the weather forecast to anticipate external effects on temperatures.

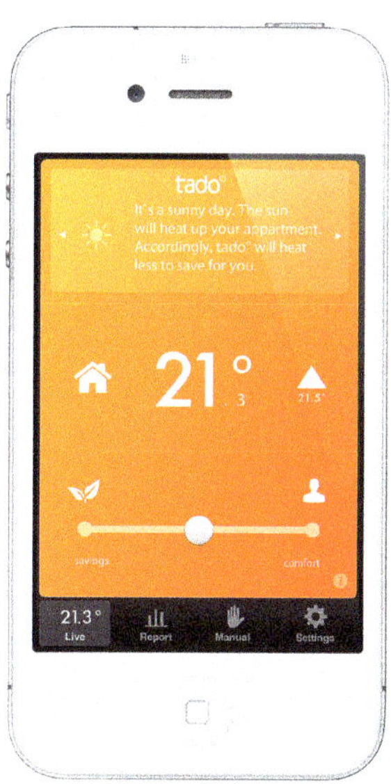
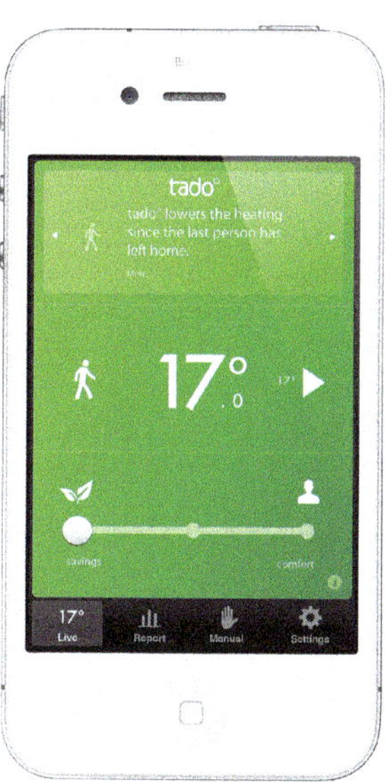
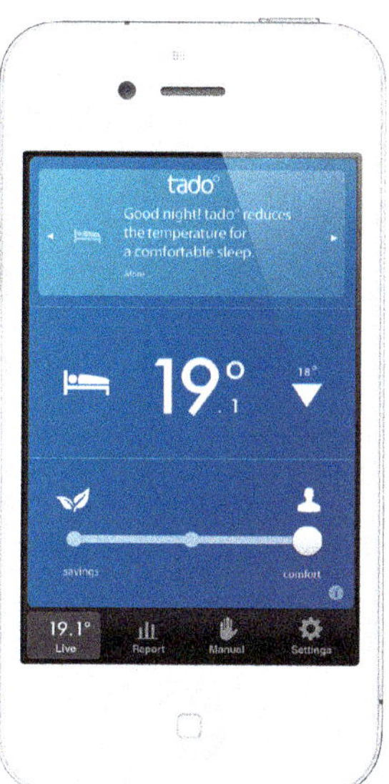
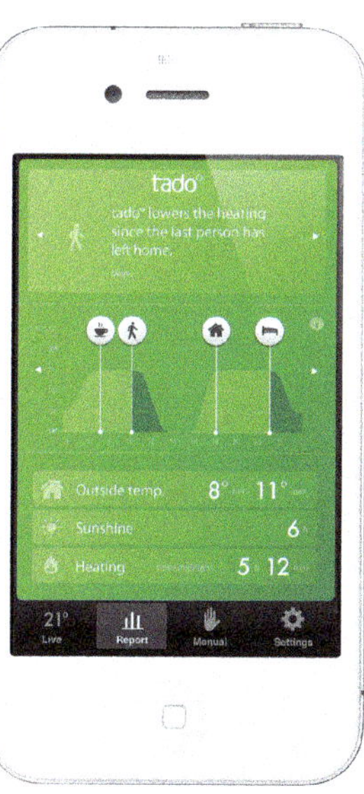

Transformed Stacking Vessels
Utopia and Utility
(Pia Wüstenberg)

Glass, wood, ceramic
Various sizes

www.utopiaandutility.eu

Utopia and Utility's Transformed Stacking Vessels are a union of glass, turned wood and ceramics, combining the work of traditional craftsmen and craft processes to create a contemporary aesthetic.

A series of functional sculptures for the home, the vessels consist of three individual containers, which stack to form the overall shape. The pieces are large and technically challenging to make, involving the expertise of wood turners in Finland, Austria, Germany and the UK, ceramicists in the UK, a ceramic engineer in Germany, and glass blowers in Finland, the Czech Republic and the UK.

Unexpanded Polystyrene Boxes
Mark Vaarwerk

Found polystyrene
Various sizes

www.vaarwerk.com
www.19greekstreet.com

Mark Vaarwerk specializes in creating products derived from thrown-away everyday materials – particularly those considered to be 'ugly'. These are objects such as computer keyboards, which are melted down to make glazes, and even cigarette ends, which can be distilled for their pigment.

The Unexpanded Polystyrene Box is in fact created from expanded polystyrene in the form of used food boxes, often found in bins at the back of restaurants. To transform this waste into useful objects, Vaarwerk uses acetone vapour as a solvent to gradually deflate the polystyrene beads, creating a much more durable material, until the boxes eventually shrink to around half of their original size.

The Energy Collection
Marjan van Aubel

Glass, solar cells
Various sizes

www.marjanvanaubel.com

The Energy Collection is a solar glassware set that gathers energy from ambient light. Regardless of whether a glass is in use or left to one side, it is constantly working to gather energy through integrated solar cells. This makes them much more efficient for use inside the home compared to standard solar panels, which only work in direct sunlight and are not suitable for indoor use.

When a glass is put away, the specially designed cabinet collects and stores the gathered energy. Working like a battery, the cabinet can then be used to charge a phone or power a light source. The technology is based on the process of photosynthesis in plants and uses a photo-sensitive dye extracted from the juice of blueberries or spinach. When the dye is struck by light it generates an electronic current.

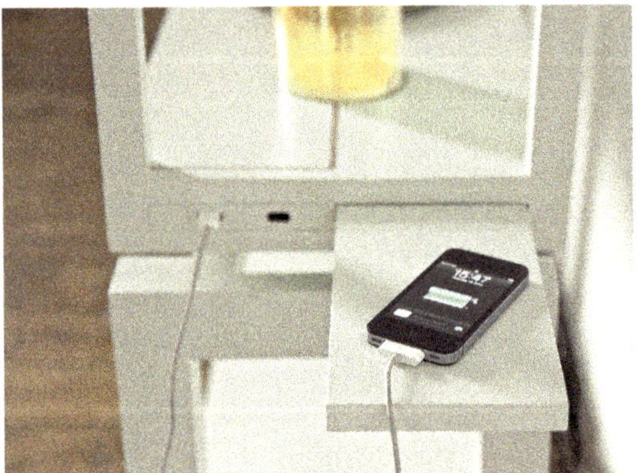

6:1
Kirstie van Noort

Ceramic
Various sizes

www.kirstievannoort.nl

The 6:1 collection by Dutch ceramicist Kirstie van Noort consists of seven cups and bowls.

The production of 1 kg (2 lb) of immaculate porcelain creates 6 kg (13 lb) of waste, and it is this ratio that gives the collection its name. Van Noort became aware of the destructive and inefficient nature of the porcelain process during a visit to Cornwall, England, where the removal of huge quantities of ore has caused permanent and large-scale damage to the landscape.

In an attempt to highlight the beauty of the waste material, six of the pieces are textured earthenware made from the coarse, pinkish brown waste, while one piece is pure porcelain white.

Incalmo Glasses
Vert Design
(Andrew Simpson)

Recycled solar panels
Various sizes

www.vertdesign.com.au

Andrew Simpson's Incalmo glasses are a collection of hand-blown vases and vessels in a range of colours, made from recycled solar panels. Created using white sand from Tasmania, the solar glass sheeting is especially difficult to work with as it is very fine.

Incalmo is a sophisticated glassmaking technique where two separate pieces are joined seamlessly, allowing two different colours in the same object.

Simpson hopes that people appreciate the pieces primarily as an attractive piece of design, rather than just a sustainable one, believing that relying on waste and recycled materials does not have to translate into bland design.

Black Ruby
Debbie Wijskamp for Serax

Recycled tyres, polyurethane binder
Various sizes

www.debbiewijskamp.com
www.serax.com

Black Ruby is a series of pots and bowls by Dutch designer Debbie Wijskamp, made using rubber powder derived from recycled car tyres.

Wijskamp specializes in handcrafting designs that explore new uses for everyday materials. Working from her Arnhem studio, she has developed a new way of mixing the powder with glue to create small pebbles. These can then be used as individual building blocks while they are still sticky, creating new objects piece by piece.

Paperpulp Vases
Debbie Wijskamp for Serax

Recycled paper, water-based binder
Various sizes

www.debbiewijskamp.com
www.serax.com

Taking inspiration from different cultures who make their homes with locally sourced materials, Dutch designer Debbie Wijskamp began to create her own building material by pulping discarded newspapers, an abundant local resource.

These surprisingly strong and waterproof Paperpulp Vases from the Serax Maison D'Etre collection, are one result of this experiment and demonstrate the material's characteristic appearance and structure.

By using sheets with differing amounts of ink coverage, it is possible to vary the colours of the finished products.

Sycamore Vessels
Tim Willey

Charred sycamore
Various sizes

timwilley.com

These simple vessels by Tim Willey are made from sycamore cut from his own woodland in North Norfolk, England. Willey manages 12 acres (5 hectares) of forest, providing him with a continuous supply of sustainable materials, which he cuts on site before transporting them back to his workshop in a wheelbarrow.

Using a lathe, Willey creates each vessel as a single piece with an integral handle, resulting in a strong and seamless design. Once shaped, the vessels are flame-charred and rubbed back to give a smooth and striking appearance.

Wonderbag
Wonderbag
(Sarah Collins)

Recycled polystyrene beads, cotton
Approx. H: 45 cm (17¾ in), W: 45 cm (17¾ in), D: 25 cm (9⅞ in)
Works with 2–9 l (2–9½ qt) pots with short handles

nb-wonderbag.com

The Wonderbag is a non-electric, insulated cooking bag filled with recycled polystyrene beads that allows food to continue cooking for hours after it has been removed from a heat source.

Developed to ease the social, economic and environmental problems associated with the simple act of preparing meals, the Wonderbag cuts fuel usage, saving money and reducing CO_2 emissions. It also saves precious water as it restricts evaporation, and avoids the burning and wastage of scarce food that can happen with stoves or open fires. Even kitchen accidents are cut down, as stoves are in use for less time and produce fewer toxic fumes, reducing respiratory diseases endemic to poorly ventilated homes.

The company runs a 'buy-one-give-one' model, donating a Wonderbag to humanitarian relief projects in South Africa for every one sold.

Raw Earth
Zuperzozial

Bamboo fibre, corn powder, natural resin
Various sizes

www.zuperzozial.com

The Zuperzozial Raw Earth collection is a range of biodegradable, durable tableware with a speckled, earthy look – made entirely of natural materials. The main ingredient is bamboo fibre, sustainably grown in China without the use of pesticides or fertilizers. There is also an organic resin binder and a small quantity of corn powder, creating a smooth surface and fine texture.

Raw Earth tableware uses only natural dyes, yet is available in a multitude of vivid colours, supporting Zuperzozial's ambition to show that living sustainably can be joyful and fun.

To make their pieces even more environmentally friendly, each item comes with no packaging other than a recycled paper label containing product information.

Airopack · Bambu · Calfee Design · Cardboard
Technologies · Carve · Craftwoods · Oscar Diaz ·
Doe · Drift · Rachel Eardley · Eco-Kids · Fine Cell
Work · Fuseproject · Tamasyn Gambell · Grain ·
Tom Hatfield · Karina Kallio · Merel Karhof ·
KeepCup · Louise Knoppert, Flore de Maillard,
Amanda Österlin La Mont & Christian Frank Müller ·
Krejci · MTA · Oeuf · Plasticana · Reality Studio ·
Rekindle · Sweet Marcel · Toto Knits · Marijn
Van Der Poll · Veja · Vert Design · Waarmakers ·
WearPanda · Ig Wilkinson · Young Ju Do

Personal Accessories

Airopack
Airopack

PET plastic
Various sizes

www.airopack.com

Airopack is a recyclable plastic universal dispensing system intended as an alternative to traditional aerosols. Although aerosols no longer contain ozone-depleting CFCs, they still rely on chemicals that contribute to global warming and emit polluting volatile organic compounds (VOCs).

Instead of these damaging propellants, Airopack relies on harmless compressed air, using 42 per cent less energy and emitting 74 per cent less CO_2. This also resolves additional problems relating to aerosols, such as solvent abuse and explosive volatility.

Airopack can be produced at low cost as it does not require the expensive machinery needed to fill aerosols slowly through the nozzle. In addition, the use of transparent plastics allows its contents to be visible to the consumer.

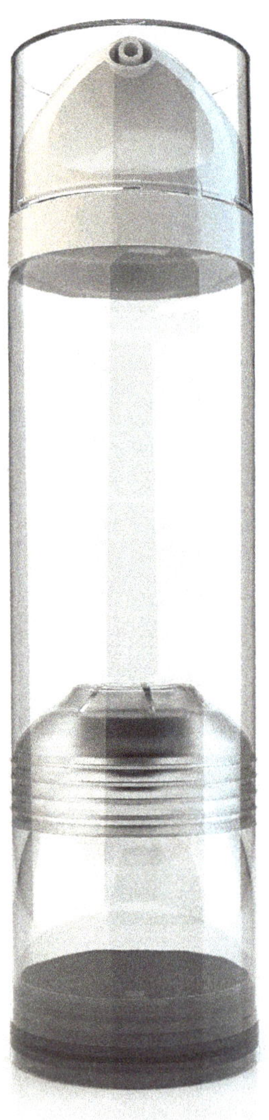

iPad Travel Case
Bambu

Sustainable cork, unbleached cotton, coconut
H: 26 cm (10¼ in), W: 21.5 cm (8½ in)

www.bambuhome.com

Bambu is a company founded by a husband-and-wife team who aspire to unite the sustainable manufacturing ethos of their native Oregon with the indigenous resources endemic to China. Products such as their handmade iPad travel case combine sustainable materials with local craftsmanship and fairtrade practices.

The case is made from sustainable cork fabric, which is naturally water- and wear-resistant, and lined with unbleached cotton. Contents are held safely inside with a waxed cotton tie, and its buttons are fashioned from coconut shell.

For more on Bambu, see the Q&A on page 186.

Bamboo Bicycle
Calfee Design (Craig Calfee)

Bamboo
Custom sizes

calfeedesign.com

Beginning as a publicity stunt in 1995, US frame builder Craig Calfee's bamboo errand bike was so popular it was eventually put into production. Available as a road bike, an MTB and even a tandem, the frames are simply made from lengths of sustainably harvested bamboo, bound by lugs made from pounded bark cloth and treated with a plant-based eco resin. Apart from its unique appearance, the frame is notable for its vibration-dampening qualities, providing a smoother ride than comparable frames of carbon, steel or aluminium.

Calfee claims, 'If there were an award for "Bicycle with lowest carbon footprint", this frame would win, hands down.' The bike is also shipped rather than flown to outlets worldwide to boost its eco-friendliness.

Cardboard Bicycle
Cardboard Technologies
(Izhar Gafni)

Cardboard, recycled plastic, recycled rubber
Weight: Less than 12 kg (27 lb)
Suitable for H: 155–190 cm (5–6 ft)
Maximum load: 125 kg (275 lb)

www.cardboardtech.com

The Cardboard Bicycle is composed of 99 per cent recycled material, 90 per cent of which is recycled cardboard, with the remaining part made of recycled plastic bottles and recycled car tyres. The bike contains no metal parts and the cardboard is protected by a waterproof resin that makes it weatherproof. Each bicycle can hold up to 1236 kg (300 lb) in weight, as a result of a patented method of folding and strengthening the cardboard.

The Cardboard Bicycle costs only $9 to manufacture and is built using a simple assembly process that can be performed by a handicapped or senior workforce.

Wooden Toys
Craftwoods (Mark Heaney) for Makers & Brothers

Walnut, ash, maple, beech, oak
Bus, H: 12 cm (4¾ in), W: 20.5 cm (8 in), D: 6.5 cm (2½ in)

craftwoods.ie
www.makersandbrothers.com

This small collection of toys is handcrafted and designed by Mark Heaney in County Sligo, Ireland, for his Craftwoods brand.

Made from a range of woods sourced in Ireland and the UK, the toys use the different shades and grains of walnut, ash, maple, beech and oak to create contrasting and tactile toys. Their handcrafted charm appeals to adults and children alike.

Tube Toys
Oscar Diaz

Cardboard, rubber, bamboo, LDPE
H: 16 cm (6¼ in), W: 8.5 cm (3⅜ in)

www.oscar-diaz.net

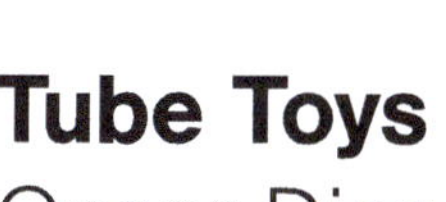 

Recognizing that children often enjoy playing with packaging as much as they do the actual toys it contains, Oscar Diaz's Tube Toys are a series of vehicles where the packaging is also part of the product.

All the parts needed to build each vehicle are contained in a cardboard tube, which doubles as the packaging and becomes the body of the car, fire engine, train or tractor. Each tube has pre-cut slots and holes to place the wheels, axles and other components.

All materials are sustainably sourced and a single paper strip displaying information and a barcode is the only disposable element. This considerably reduces the amount of material discarded after purchase, as well as the added cost of traditional packaging.

iPad Cover / Clutch
Doe

Leather
H: 17 cm (6¾ in), L: 28 cm (11 in)

www.doeleather.co.uk

Bench-made in the UK by skilled craftspeople in one of the Black Country's last remaining leather goods workshops, Doe's iPad cover and clutch bag is a simple celebration of top-quality, hand-waxed bridle hide.

Doe is an English heritage story, beginning in 1908 with current owner Deborah Thomas's great, great grandfather producing leather linings for hats and shoes. The company went on to specialize in embossing prints such as snake, lizard, crocodile and ostrich on to quality hides, and eventually held the largest collection of embossing plates in the world. Due to cheap competition from overseas, the factory ceased production in 2002 but the unique archive prints were preserved in swatch books. A selection of these is now recycled to create hand-stitched zip pulls for each new collection of bags.

Sea Glass Bracelets
Drift (Fiona Petheram)

Sea glass, 14-carat gold, silk, leather
Various sizes

www.driftjewellery.com

This bracelet by Drift is handmade by jewellery designer Fiona Petheram, using sea glass found along the coastlines of Suffolk, Spain and the Isles of Scilly, combined with semi-precious stones, precious metals, silk and leather.

Each piece is carefully selected, lightly polished and drilled by hand before being worked into a piece of jewellery. The design takes its lead from the varied sizes and sculptural shapes of the individual pieces of glass.

Petheram delights in the range of colours found in sea glass, from luminous whites, greens and blues, that were probably once part of a wine, ale or ink bottle, through to the rarer purples and pinks that perhaps come from perfume or medicine bottles. Whatever its age and origin, sea glass began its journey from something that was once discarded, maybe hundreds of years ago, or perhaps just last summer.

Coin Jewellery
Rachel Eardley

Recycled coins, silver
Various sizes

www.racheleardley.com

Rachel Eardley's jewellery is crafted from a rich supply of old coins, gathered from junk sales and flea markets.

Looking past their monetary worth, Eardley exploits her collection as a rich and diverse source of finely crafted, ready-made intricate drawings and designs. Elements such as copper wrens from British farthings and brass owls from Greek drachmas are meticulously cut from their backgrounds before being smoothed, polished and finished with silver, ready to fulfil new roles on rings, brooches and necklaces.

Eco-Dough
Eco-Kids

Organic fruit, plant and vegetable extracts
5 x 115 g (4 oz) containers

www.ecokidsusa.com

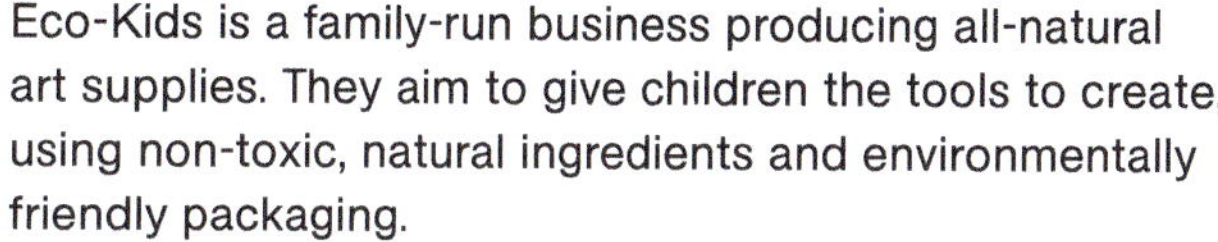

Eco-Kids is a family-run business producing all-natural art supplies. They aim to give children the tools to create, using non-toxic, natural ingredients and environmentally friendly packaging.

Living by their mantra 'creative play the natural way', the company create their modelling product, Eco-Dough, from organic fruit, plant and vegetable extracts. Ingredients and sources include annatto seed, beets, blueberries, carrots, paprika, purple sweet potato, red cabbage, spinach, flour, salt, cream of tartar, organic rosemary oil, vitamin E oil, soybean oil, coconut oil, potassium sorbate and citric acid.

The colours of the dough are earthy yet vibrant, while essential oils keep it soft and pliable, and also provide a light aroma.

Patchwork Bags
Fine Cell Work

Fabric offcuts
Various sizes

www.finecellwork.co.uk

Combining wool, tweeds and furnishing fabric offcuts, Fine Cell Works' upcycled bags are created by prisoners in British gaols. The company trains prisoners in paid, skilled, creative needlework to foster hope, discipline and self-esteem. Learning new skills and helping support their families with the money they earn, inmates are able to connect with wider society and are given a brighter outlook on their future. Guiding prisoners towards formal work training and qualifications encourages them to leave prison with the confidence and financial means to avoid re-offending.

Providing a broad range of embroidered cushions, bags, pictures and patchwork quilts, the work is of high quality as prisoners are taught and supported by volunteers from the Embroiderers' Guild and the Quilters' Guild.

Whole World Water Bottle
Fuseproject (Yves Behar)
with Whole World Water

Glass, recycled aluminium

wholeworldwater.co

This glass bottle by Fuseproject's Yves Behar
is the icon of the Whole World Water campaign, an
enterprise to provide universal access to clean and safe
water. The bottles are made of extra-thick glass in order
to survive many cycles of washing and reuse, and the
recycled aluminium cap is similarly reusable.

The project encourages hospitality and catering
companies to filter, bottle and sell their own tap water
in order to eliminate unnecessary food miles and plastic
wastage, while also saving money. Ten per cent of these
proceeds are then channelled by the Whole World
Water Fund into supporting water programmes around
the world.

It is hoped that the hospitality and tourism industry can
contribute $1 billion per year to the campaign, providing
vital assistance to the almost 1 billion people around the
world without access to safe drinking water.

Notebooks
Tamasyn Gambell

Recycled card and paper, vegetable inks
H: 21 cm (8¼ in), W: 14.8 cm (5⅞ in)

www.tamasyngambell.com

Frustrated with the amount of waste and the fast pace of the fashion industry, Tamasyn Gambell started up her own company in 2008, focusing on considered prints and timeless design, using the most environmentally friendly processes possible. All her materials are locally sourced and production runs are kept small to minimize waste.

These A5-size notebooks comprise recycled card covers with pages made up of rejected paper sheets. The bold, graphic cover designs are printed by a socially responsible cooperative in London using vegetable inks.

Bound Hand V1
Grain (James & Chelsea Minola)

Mirrored clear glass, FSC-certified birch, hemp twine
H: 24.6 cm (9⅝ in), W: 12.7 cm (5 in), D: 1.3 cm (½ in)

www.graindesign.com

Seattle-based design house Grain aim to unite current manufacturing technologies and age-old craft techniques. This approach is typified in the manufacture of their Bound Mirrors, which combine precision-crafted parts with intensively hand-wrapped, tactile twine.

Comprising a section of waterjet-cut salvaged mirror glass backed with a matching sheet of FSC-certified birch, the colourful hand mirrors are then bound together with hemp twine in the Grain design studio on Bainbridge Island in the Pacific Northwest.

Q&A: Grain

Chelsea and James Minola met while studying industrial design at the Rhode Island School of Design in Providence, USA. Before that, James studied and worked in boat building in Maine and Chelsea studied and worked in interior design in New York. Together they run Grain, a practice focused on linking design and sustainability.

www.graindesign.com

Inspired by James's past experience as a boatbuilder in Maine, Hung is an oval-shaped waterjet-cut mirror threaded and hung by manila rope.

How would you describe your style?

We usually start with some basic idea – a solution for something or an inventive way to work with a specific material or manufacturing technique – over a style. That said, there is a visual cleanliness to most of our finished work that does begin to unify everything as a collection. This unity is important as we build our body of work.

In what way is your work sustainable?

To the best of our ability, we run a socially and environmentally responsible design business. This way of working includes thoughtful design of our products – including material use, production and life cycle – as well as packaging and printing. We are also mindful of shipping, our studio environment, the employees and artisans with whom we work, giving back through our 1% For The Planet commitment, and engaging with local and national organizations supporting emerging design and design education.

What material sand techniques do you use?

We aren't rooted in any one material or technique. This is a conscious choice, as we want to keep ourselves open to new discoveries. Recently, we have begun exploring ceramics and have several new ideas for both hand-built and slip-cast products using terracotta clay.

Are there any particular designers or artists that inspire you?

Over the past several years we have gained a lot of inspiration from working with several textile artisan communities in Guatemala. We are currently working with a community that is producing all our naturally dyed threads. They source local plants, flowers and barks to help us realize all the colours. It is a process that is a mix between cooking and magic, and we are so in awe.

Have you noticed any particular trends in sustainable design?

There does seem to be a renewed emphasis on design with a more seamless integration of sustainable practices and materials. Locally, we are also seeing more designers adopting small-batch manufacturing. Many of the designers we admire are engaging in more sustainable practices even if they are not calling their work 'sustainable design'. This is a great sign that these ideas are becoming more of a requirement of good design than an extra.

What materials or techniques do you think we'll be seeing more of in the future?

Natural materials will always be of interest to designers. It is our hope that improvements to the management of these resources will continue to grow.

Many of Grain's products are produced in collaboration with artisan communities in Guatemala, including a group who produce and weave naturally dyed yarn.

Sololá Zipper
Grain (James & Chelsea Minola)

Recycled cotton
Various sizes

www.graindesign.com

The Sololá purse by Grain Design upcycles vintage textiles to create a unique mix of colour and craft, while supporting sustainable incomes for artisans in Guatemala. The purses are made from huipils (traditional women's blouses woven on a backstrap loom) sourced at a local market and assembled nearby.

By exposing the reverse side of the weave, each one-of-a-kind purse celebrates the techniques and individual aesthetics of Guatemalan women weavers.

Banner Bags
Tom Hatfield

Recycled banners
L: 60 cm (23⅝ in), Diam.: 20 cm (7⅞ in)

www.tomhatfield.co.uk

London-based designer Tom Hatfield's Banner Bags make use of the type of nylon banners seen lining the streets during marathons. Although this strong and colourful material is suitable for a range of recycling applications, Hatfield gives it a particularly appropriate new life as a sports bag, thereby helping its owner train for their next race.

The protoype of the bag was auctioned to raise money for the art department of a local children's school.

Christmas Tree Sledge
Tom Hatfield

Christmas trees
H: 38 cm (15 in), L: 100 cm (39⅜ in), W: 40 cm (15¾ in)

www.tomhatfield.co.uk

Tom Hatfield's sledge is made from the discarded post-season Christmas trees found on the streets of London every year. After being trimmed and sawn to length, the parts are assembled using traditional woodcraft techniques for working green wood (wood that has not been dried or seasoned first).

Hatfield decided that with snowy weather becoming a more regular occurrence, this sledge seemed an appropriate marriage of design and abundant materials. Being such an iconic, seasonal object, a sledge is the perfect symbol of the wastefulness of consigning millions of trees to landfill after just two weeks of use.

Kallio Clothing
Karina Kallio

Recycled cotton
Various sizes

kallionyc.com

Kallio clothing was conceived as a response to the ubiquity of mass production, throwaway culture and excess in general. Rather than continuing to contribute to this situation, founder Karina Kallio left her job in commercial fashion to establish her own sustainable brand for children. The designs are made entirely from reclaimed vintage cotton and flannel men's shirts, resewn in ethical factories and given new life.

Kallio's vision is to create 'a conscious kid's fashion brand that is fun, stylish and unexpected, that kids can play hard in, without being hard on the environment.'

Wind Knitted Scarves
Merel Karhof

Wool
Various sizes

www.merelkarhof.nl

Dutch designer Merel Karhof's 'Wind Knitting Factory' is a wind-powered knitting machine, inspired by the traditional windmills of her native country (see page 76). This mobile wind factory is intended to demonstrate what can be produced with the free and inexhaustible energy source of urban wind.

How fast the machine knits is dependent on how windy it is. The fabric it produces is periodically harvested and transformed into a range of objects such as scarves. Each scarf is given a label bearing the time and date on which it was knitted, as well as the number of minutes it took.

Movers and Shakers
KeepCup

Polypropylene
227, 340 or 454 ml (8, 12 or 16 oz)

www.keepcup.com

KeepCup's mission is to encourage the use of reusable cups and to change the way we think about convenience culture, initiating the demise of the disposable. Their Movers and Shakers cups need only be used 15 times to break even with paper cups in terms of the energy used in manufacture, and because most disposable cups are lined with plastic, they cannot be recycled.

Movers and Shakers are ergonomic, unbreakable and dishwasher safe, but if they do come to the end of their life, they are completely recyclable. Additionally, they are lightweight and stackable, keeping the environmental costs of shipping and freight low. The ability to ship components for local assembly also decreases the environmental impact of the KeepCup.

Animal Coffin

Louise Knoppert,
Flore de Maillard,
Amanda Österlin La Mont
& Christian Frank Müller

Various organic materials
Various sizes

www.adream2012.eu

The biodegradable Animal Coffin offers an ecologically sound option to meet the increasing demand for pet funerals.

After a number of experiments with materials, the designers settled on a combination of substances including starch, flour, cardboard, coffee grounds, vinegar and hair. This ensures the compostability of the product, and at the same time provides the necessary sturdiness and aesthetics appropriate for a coffin.

The lid of the coffin contains seeds to enable a tree to grow on the site of the burial, providing a long-lasting, eco-friendly memorial. The animal and coffin alike provide effective nutrients for the young growing tree.

Tubus
Krejci (Doreen Westphal)

Used inner tubes
Various sizes

www.doreenwestphal.com
krejci.fr

Receiving a bag full of inner tubes as a joke Christmas present, former tailor Doreen Westphal immediately saw potential in the raw material and set about stitching together her first inner-tube bags.

After much experimentation and research, this became the Tubus series, a line of strong, unique-looking bags based on original Amsterdam bicycle inner tubes, lined with coloured felt.

The bags are produced in Poland by disabled workers, from an endless supply of discarded inner tubes. Westphal's company Krejci has calculated that in Holland 10,000 tubes are incinerated as waste per day.

Tepuy & Roraima
MTA (Maria Teresa Aristeguieta)

Amazonian hardwoods, semi-precious stones, silver plate
H: 6.5 cm (2½ in), W: 19.5 cm (7⅝ in), D: 11.5 cm (4½ in)

www.mtabags.com

Tepuy (left) and Roraima (right) are a pair of wooden clutch bags designed and handcrafted in Venezuela. Incorporating a diverse range of contrasting indigenous hardwoods, Maria Teresa Aristeguieta's designs are created using elaborate and exacting handcarving techniques by native artisans in the Amazonian rainforest.

In collaboration with the local community, MTA have developed a small plantation system in order to prevent illegal logging and to create sustainable wood production. All profits from the sale of these wooden clutches go directly to the native artisans.

Goodies
Oeuf

Alpaca
Various sizes

www.oeufnyc.com

New York's Oeuf brand makes every effort to ensure that their manufacturing processes respect both artisans and the environment.

This collection of playful knitted accesseories is handcrafted in 100 per cent baby alpaca, a luxurious, hypo-allergenic and sustainable material. Each of the fun designs is made by a cooperative of Bolivian artisans, where women are able to practise their art in a favourable working environment, enabling them to afford healthcare and education for their children.

Plasticana Shoes
Plasticana

Recycled plastics, hemp, sugar, pectin
Various sizes

www.plasticana.com

Plasticana shoes are made in France from a blend of recycled plastics and locally grown hemp fibre. Hemp plants are very productive in absorbing carbon from the atmosphere and are central to the company's aim to reduce dependency on oil-based plastics. The result is a completely recyclable, sustainable material with a distinctive golden brown colour, caused by sugars in the mixture being heated during the thermal molding process.

Every pair of Plasticana shoes comes packaged in its own bag, made of compostable materials.

Souvenir Collection
Reality Studio (Svenja Specht)

Nubuck leather, cork
Various sizes

www.realitystudio.de

Inspired by souvenirs and objects brought home from distant travels, Reality Studio's Souvenir collection of shoes aims to keep the memory of holidays alive.

Designer Svenja Specht is heavily influenced by traditional clothing, made using ancient craft techniques, and is wary of disposable fashion and wasteful mass-production methods. This is why her Berlin-based fashion label chose to manufacture their line of cork shoes in a small factory in Portugal. Portugal has a centuries-old tradition of working with sustainable cork and provides a third of the total output worldwide. Industrial cork plantations absorb significant amounts of carbon from the atmosphere, as stripping the cork every decade allows a new and more absorbent coat to grow.

Offcut Inlaid Bracelet
Rekindle with Jeremy Leeming

Reclaimed wood, silver or gold
Inside diam.: 6.5 or 7 cm (2½ or 2¾ in)

rekindle.org.nz

Rekindle is a social enterprise in New Zealand that actively enables youth to gain real and transferable work skills making furniture and other products from waste wood, much of which comes from homes irreparably damaged by the earthquake in 2011. Some of this timber is from ancient, slow-growing indigenous species, felled in the early twentieth century, but which are now protected and will never again be available (see also page 93).

Using offcuts of this material, augmented with precious metals by Christchurch jeweller Jeremy Leeming, these inlaid bracelets celebrate this precious timber, which might otherwise have been discarded or burnt.

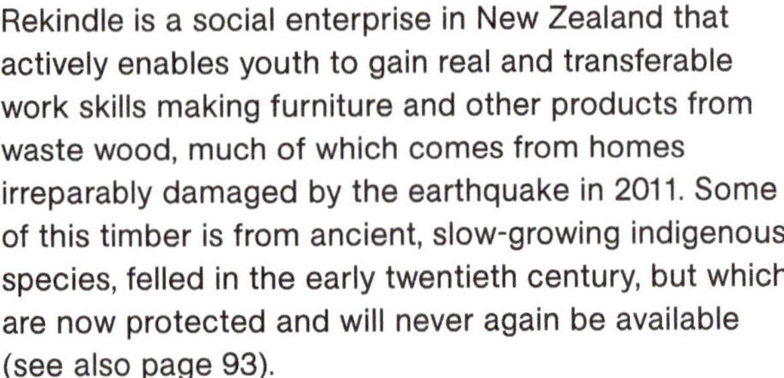

Socks
Sweet Marcel
(Amy Anderson)

Recycled cotton
Various sizes

www.sweetmarcel.com

Sweet Marcel's socks are made in the US from recycled cotton yarn, giving new life to unwanted textiles. Founded by Amy Anderson in Texas, the company draws its design inspiration from close observation of the natural world and experiences of the globe's varied cultures.

The socks are packaged entirely in recycled materials.

Animal Knits
Toto Knits

Organic cotton, wool, bio-friendly dyes
Various sizes

www.totoknits.com

Toto Knits are ethically produced in Kenya by a group of local artisans. They encourage trade, rather than aid, to help local single mothers learn new skills and work in a flexible way that fits around their family responsibilities. The company trains and manages a group of up to 200 knitters, making designs for children inspired by their local surroundings in the African bush.

Taking its name from the Swahili word *mtoto*, meaning 'child', the collections are handmade from locally grown organic cotton and wool from neighbouring Uganda. They are then coloured using natural dyes.

OS Suitcase
Marijn Van Der Poll
for OpenStructures

Aluminium, steel, wood, polyester
H: 41.9 cm (16½ in), L: 56 cm (22 in), W: 2 cm (¾ in)

www.marijnvanderpoll.com
intrastructures.net
openstructures.net

This suitcase is part of the OpenStructures (OS) project, a construction system where designers create interchangeable components on a shared modular grid (see page 227). These products can then be recycled or traded, avoiding unnecessary waste.

The main body of the case is made from BlocBox parts, designed by Thomas Lomée and Jo Van Bostraeten. This versatile component is also used in such diverse designs as swings, sledges and bike baskets.

The ultimate goal is to create a common open standard, allowing the broadest range of people, from craftsmen to multinationals, to design, build and exchange the widest range of modular components, resulting in a more flexible and scalable built environment.

Shoes
Veja

Organic cotton, leather, sheepskin, natural rubber
Various sizes

www.veja-store.com

French manufacturer Veja aims to create shoes that combine principles of economic, social and environmental development, creating a positive chain from the producers to the consumers.

In sourcing its raw materials, the company works with a cooperative of *seringueiros* (rubber tappers) in the heart of the Amazonian rainforest. Veja buys their rubber at a premium price, allowing them to live decently from rubber tapping, reducing the financial appeal of land clearance. All Veja's cotton is certified organic and their leather is free from heavy metals, tanned with acacia extracts and dyed with vegetable inks.

In France, the company has built a partnership with the social association Ateliers Sans Frontières, which helps to reintegrate people back into society through work. This association takes care of the storage and delivery of Veja's collections.

BioPak Biodegradable Packaging
Vert Design (Andrew Simpson) with BioPak

Bamboo pulp, sugarcane pulp
Holds 25 wipes, each 20 x 18 cm (7⅞ x 7⅛ in)

www.vertdesign.com.au
www.biopak.com.au
www.wotnot.com.au

Wotnot wipes are packaged in a sustainable dispenser, designed by Andrew Simpson of Vert Design and manufactured by BioPak, an Australian specialist in environmentally friendly packaging products.

BioPak's goal is to influence change by promoting packaging made from a range of annually renewable, biodegradable resources that seamlessly replace oil-based packaging, without adding cost or requiring consumers to think or act differently. The company believe that if given an economically viable and cost-effective choice, the status quo will go green. Wotnot wipes themselves use natural and organic ingredients, cleanse and moisturize skin, and are manufactured using 100 per cent renewable energy in the company's office and warehouse.

All waste is either reused or recycled, and a percentage of all Wotnot sales are donated to the Bear Cottage children's hospice in New South Wales.

Q&A: Veja

In 2003, Sébastien Kopp and Ghislain Morillion, founders of footware and accessories company Veja, travelled around the world studying sustainable development projects. Veja is the result of this adventure. Now, working with cooperatives of small farmers across Brazil, Veja uses organic and fair trade cotton, wild Amazonian rubber and naturally tanned leather to create products that respect both the environment and every worker involved.

www.veja-store.com

Veja produce organic and fair-trade footwear and accessories.

How would you describe your style?

Veja strives to offer a different vision that combines fashion, fair trade and ecology and links together economy, social initiatives and the environment. It is a vision that proposes cultural change. From the fields of raw materials in Brazil to the doors of the fashion stores in Europe where our sneakers and accessories are available, Veja respects very high social and environmental standards. This means a thorough involvement in agro-ecology farming initiatives in North Brazil, in deforestation fighting in the Amazon, in workers' rights and dignity protection and also in social rehabilitation projects back in Europe.

In what way is your work sustainable?

Since its inception in 2004, Veja has been using agro-ecological cotton to craft sneakers (see page 306). The cotton used in the canvas of the sneakers is grown by an association of small-scale farmers located in one of Brazil's poorest areas, Ceará, in the northeast of the country. Here, in contrast to the predominant monoculture farming system in northeast Brazil, small producers grow cotton and food crops under agro-ecology principles, which ban the use of agro-chemicals and pesticides. For those small-scale farmers (1 hectare of land on average), farming development goes hand-in-hand with environmental protection.

Preserving the Amazonian rainforest is one of the main goals of Veja. The rubber used in the soles of Veja sneakers comes from the Amazon, the only place on earth where rubber trees grow in the wild. Veja works with a cooperative of 36 families of seringueiros (rubber tappers) who harvest the rubber for the soles of Veja sneakers in the Chico Mendes reserve. Veja buys rubber from the seringueiros at a premium, allowing them to live on rubber harvesting with dignity. They are thus less tempted by the financial opportunities of land-clearing, cattle breeding or wood extraction. For Veja, supporting rubber tapping means that large areas of forest are protected and the local biodiversity is preserved.

We are also concerned about Veja's global carbon footprint. The trainers are shipped from Porto Alegre, Brazil, to Le Havre, France, and then travel by barge to Paris. The shoe boxes are made of recycled and recyclable cardboard, while Enercoop, a renewable-energy company, powers our headquarters. To offset CO_2 emissions that can't be further reduced, we take part in a tree-planting initiative in Peru called Pure Project.

Have you noticed any particular trends in sustainable design?

We believe the real trend in sustainable design is to focus on timeless, useful and long-lasting products. What is more sustainable than an object or a cloth that you can keep on using from generation to generation? Sustainable design is meant to change consumption habits and to reduce the amount of products that we buy or need.

What materials or techniques do you think we'll be seeing more of in the future?

After investing in all sorts of chemical and synthetic combinations, we are re-exploring the amazing properties of natural materials or ancestral techniques. It is true with leather. For example, we banned the use of chrome or heavy metals to tan our leather, and instead use plant extracts such as acacia. In a way, this is going back to the ancient traditions of leather tanning. Other examples are Ventile cotton or Merino wool. Ventile cotton is 100% natural and widely used today for its waterproof and windproof but breathable, durable and quiet properties.

Preserving the Amazonian rainforest is one of Veja's main goals. The company works with a cooperative of families who harvest rubber sustainably.

Be.e
Waarmakers (Maarten Heijltjes & Simon Akkaya) for Van.Eko

Flax, cellulose
H (including windscreen): 145 cm (57⅛ in)

waarmakers.nl
vaneko.com

The Be.e is an electric bio-scooter designed by design duo Waarmakers (Maarten Heijltjes and Simon Akkaya) for Van.Eko. The monocoque body is made from Dutch flax and bio-resin and is so strong that it does not need an internal frame, saving considerable weight.

The scooter can be leased from Van.Eko with a sharing plan, whereby the primary user can offer it to other registered users when it is not in use. The company want the scooter to be used as much as possible in its lifetime, creating the highest possible ratio of raw material to kilometres ridden, rather than left sitting in a garage.

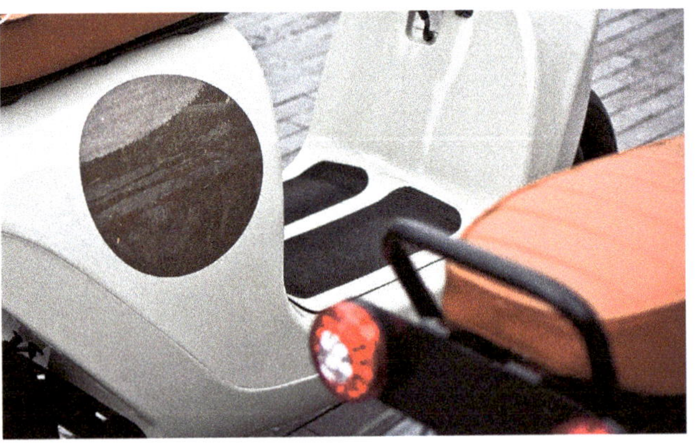

WearPanda Sunglasses
WearPanda

Bamboo, recycled polycarbonates
Various sizes

wearpanda.com

WearPanda is a luxury sunglasses brand aiming to increase the social responsibility of business. In partnership with the TOMA (Tribal Outreach Medical Assistance) Foundation, the company provide a free eye or medical exam to a person in need for every pair sold. They also donate a pair of prescription glasses or sunglasses (for those with cataracts or a similar type of eye deficiency).

The sunglasses themselves have lenses of recycled polycarbonate and frames handcrafted from sustainable bamboo. Bamboo is an ideal material for sunglasses as it is flexible, yet stronger than even some alloys of steel.

Ig Wood Surfboards
Ig Wilkinson

Wood
Various sizes

www.igwoodsurf.com

Based on the Atlantic coast of Devon, England, surfer and shaper Ig Wilkinson specializes in environmentally friendly custom board designs, from longboards to shortboards and everything in between.

Reacting against the overwhelming use of toxic chemicals and plastics in industrial surfboard construction, Ig Wood surfboards are made exclusively from sustainable timber using trees fallen within a 20-mile radius of Wilkinson's workshop. Using only hand tools, each board is shaped and assembled with the minimum of glue, and finished with natural oils and varnishes.

Compostable Accessories
Young Ju Do

Organic matter
Various sizes

art-ju.com

This collection of Compostable Accessories is Young Ju Do's response to the question of how biodegradability can be considered as a key feature for design, prompting people to take a fresh look at the issues of short-term use.

Many biodegradable products can only be broken down in an industrial composting facility; this project, therefore, aimed to create personal accessories that were home-degradable as well as being biologically nutritious.

This meant creating a carefully balanced composition of 'brown' and 'green' bio-matter that could decompose at the end of its life without negative effects, while also providing food for bacteria and microbiological life.

Index

Names in bold indicate Q&A features

Index

Index

Photo Credits

10: gnam box
11: Gerrit Meier
20: Grandpeople www.grandpeople.no
22 (top): Magne Sandes www.magnesandes.no
22 (bottom): Grandpeople www.grandpeople.no
37 (top): Vera Cannone
37 (bottom): Mirco Cecchi
39: Jamie McGregor Smith and Yoav Reches
40 (top left): Joshua Hoffman /
   Joshua Hoffman Photo
42: Frank Tielemans Fotografie BV
44 (left): Cristóbal Marambio – All rights reserved
   www.cristobalmarambio.com
44 (right): PECAS
47: Studio CafeNoir
51: Hironori Tsukue
53: Peter Van Dijk
61: Discipline www.discipline.eu
71 (bottom): Ben Blood – All Rights Reserved
90: Jamie McGregor Smith and Yoav Reches
91: Jamie McGregor Smith and Yoav Reches
92: Laura Forest
99: Julian Lechner
101 (bottom left): Veronica Gaido
105: Jon Gooding
109 (left, top right): Petr Krejci
110 (bottom): Wai Ming Nig
112: Rogier Arients
120: Marc Eden Schooley
124: Studio Badini Createam – Viadana MN – Italy
136: Ett La Benn
137: www.diephotodesigner.de
138 (top): Ailine Liefeld Photography,
   @ Studio138, Torstr. 138, 10119 Berlin,
   http://ailineliefeld.com
138 (bottom): Ett La Benn
139: Ett La Benn

140 (left): Alan J. Crossley
140 (right): John Valls
141: Discipline www.discipline.eu
143: Tim Stet
144: Tim Stet
148: Annemarijneepep Bonet
149: Pep Bonet
158: Aaron Van Holland
164: Nick Rochowski
167: Sameli Rantanen
186 (top): Mick Ryan
205: Sjoerd Eickmans fotografie
206: Sjoerd Eickmans fotografie
208: Boone Speed
209: Ett La Benn
210 (bottom): Boone Speed
211: Boone Speed
213: Discipline www.discipline.eu
214: Jose Manuel Varela Vela
223: Pep Bonet
224 (top): Ed Kulakowski
229: Hironori Tsukue
230: Jeremy Johns
241: Takumi Ota Photography
248 (right): Johan Hackman
249: RSVP srl, Italy
255: Eikon Studio di Gainluca Perticoni
257: Hironori Tsukue
264: Wai Ming Nig
267: Jan VD Schilden
277: Ilan Besor
280: Julia Bostock
281: Julia Bostock
287: Ben Blood – All Rights Reserved
288: Ben Blood – All Rights Reserved
290: Ben Blood – All Rights Reserved
302: Laura Forest